ORTHO'S All About

Bathroom Remodeling

Project Editor: Karen K. Johnson
Writers: Larry Hodgson and Linda Mason Hunter
Illustrators: Dave Brandon and Tony Davis

Meredith® Books
Des Moines, Iowa

Ortho® Books
An imprint of Meredith® Books

Ortho's All About Bathroom Remodeling
Editor: Larry Erickson
Art Director: Tom Wegner
Copy Chief: Catherine Hamrick
Copy and Production Editor: Terri Fredrickson
Contributing Writer: Linda Mason Hunter
Contributing Copy Editor: Carl A. Hill III
Technical Proofreader: Ken Wilkinson
Contributing Proofreader: Colleen Johnson
Electronic Production Coordinator: Paula Forest
Editorial and Design Assistants: Kathleen Stevens, Judy
    Bailey, Kaye Chabot, Treesa Landry, Karen Schirm
Production Director: Douglas M. Johnston
Production Manager: Pam Kvitne
Assistant Prepress Manager: Marjorie J. Schenkelberg

Additional Editorial Contributions from
    Art Rep Services
Director: Chip Nadeau
Designer: Laura Rades
Illustrator: Dave Brandon

Meredith® Books
Editor in Chief: James D. Blume
Design Director: Matt Strelecki
Managing Editor: Gregory H. Kayko
Executive Ortho Editor: Benjamin W. Allen

Director, Sales & Marketing, Retail: Michael A. Peterson
Director, Sales & Marketing, Special Markets:
    Rita McMullen
Director, Sales & Marketing, Home & Garden Center
    Channel: Ray Wolf
Director, Operations: George A. Susral

Vice President, General Manager: Jamie L. Martin

Meredith Publishing Group
President, Publishing Group: Christopher M. Little
Vice President, Consumer Marketing & Development:
    Hal Oringer

Meredith Corporation
Chairman and Chief Executive Officer: William T. Kerr

Chairman of the Executive Committee: E.T. Meredith III

Photographers
King Au: 23
Gordon Beall: 87
Ernest Braun Photography: 28
Ross Chapple Photography: 90
Stephen Cridland Photography: 37B, 54, 57, 76
Timothy C. Fields: 4
D. Randolph Foulds Photography: 10
Edward Gohlich Photography: cover, 35
Geoffrey Gross Photography: 25
Jamie Hadley: 18, 27
Bill Holt: 26, 58
William Hopkins Sr.: 51, 88
Linda Mason Hunter: 64
Jon Jensen: 37T
Mike Jensen: 38, 40, 78
Jenifer Jordan: 61, 86, 93
Scott Little: 62
Eric Roth: 81
William Stites: 44
Rick Taylor Photography: 17, 20, 31
John Vaughan: 52
Jessie Walker: 66
James Yochum: 8

All of us at Ortho® Books are dedicated to providing you
with the information and ideas you need to enhance your
home and garden. We welcome your comments and
suggestions about this book. Write to us at:
Meredith Corporation
Ortho Books
1716 Locust St.
Des Moines, IA 50309–3023

Note to the Readers: Due to differing conditions, tools,
and individual skills, Meredith Corporation assumes no
responsibility for any damages, injuries suffered, or losses
incurred as a result of following the information published
in this book. Before beginning any project, review the
instructions carefully, and if any doubts or questions remain,
consult local experts or authorities. Because codes and
regulations vary greatly, you always should check with
authorities to ensure that your project complies with all
applicable local codes and regulations. Always read and
observe all of the safety precautions provided by
manufacturers of any tools, equipment, or supplies,
and follow all accepted safety procedures.

Ortho® is a trademark of Monsanto Company used
under license.

FIRST STEPS

REFINING THE DESIGN

PROJECT PLANNING

CONSTRUCTION GUIDE

FIRST STEPS

Good bathroom design meets three tough criteria. It makes creative use of available space. It combines all elements into an integrated and satisfying whole. And it reflects the personal style of the people who depend on it every day.

The secret to meeting these standards lies in identifying your problems, then searching patiently and carefully for the right solutions.

Whether you're designing a new bathroom or remodeling an existing one, the design process involves the same steps:

- Surveying the existing space
- Establishing a design style
- Laying out fixture locations
- Choosing finishing materials

This chapter takes you through the first two steps and offers guidelines for planning the bathroom layout.

Preparation is the most important step in the entire process, so give yourself plenty of time. It can take weeks, even months, to design a new bathroom and prepare for construction. Even if you plan to use professional help, complete as many of the preliminary steps as possible. The project will go more smoothly if you do.

Golden yellow walls, glazed to reflect light, and black-and-white checkered tile define the upbeat personality of this bath designed for two.

RESEARCH THE PROJECT

Begin by gathering information; assessing the present bathroom; setting goals and priorities for the new room; and evaluating the realities of the remodeling project in terms of cost, codes, and the structural integrity of your home. To clarify your ideas, you must make many decisions, and you always must be ready to refine and revise your plans.

GATHER IDEAS

One of your first and most enjoyable tasks will be to gather ideas. Start with the ideas in this book, then set up a filing system to organize notes, clippings, and brochures. An accordion file works well because it will hold bulky items, such as magazines and samples of materials. Use categories suggested by the page headings and checklists in this book, or devise your own system of classification.

If you gather more ideas than you can use, don't be afraid to weed them out. Be sure to save product specifications and installation instructions you will need later.

You'll find many sources of information:
■ Home magazines available at your supermarket or newsstand (some devoted exclusively to bathrooms).
■ Trade publications distributed only to professionals. Look for these in a large library or in the office of an architect or contractor.
■ Manufacturers who can send you brochures, specification sheets, installation instructions, and lists of dealers. Look for an address or a contact in advertisements. Check your local library for a copy of *Sweet's Catalog*, a publication of building products.
■ Retail stores and showrooms.
■ Showrooms furnished by bathroom specialists, plumbing suppliers, home improvement centers, and other dealers. They may sell only to contractors and other professionals, or they may have a limited selection of brands, but they still can yield many good ideas. Ask if they have a portfolio of local bathroom projects you can browse.
■ Model homes, open houses, and home tours. Bring a tape measure and a pencil and paper so you can take notes.
■ Computer programs designed for creating and refining floor plans.
■ New or remodeled bathrooms in homes of your friends and family. Ask these homeowners what they like or dislike about various various features. If you do not intend to do all the work yourself, you can ask them to recommend qualified professionals.

ASSESS THE SPACE

While you're gathering information, examine the present bathroom. Even though it has features you don't like, it may have some qualities you want to retain. The Bathroom Survey (*on pages 10 and 11*) will help you assess your needs in terms of light, space, storage, layout, and other amenities. You need this information to create your new design.

You also will need a floor plan of the existing space (*see page 8*) to use as a starting point for new layouts. Draw up this floor plan before you do the survey. It provides an additional tool for making notes and gives you a chance to verify critical dimensions. If you work with design professionals, doing these tasks prior to the first meeting will streamline the process and make you more knowledgeable about your own project.

SET PRIORITIES

Notes you take while gathering ideas and your answers on the *Bathroom Survey* will help you set design goals for the new bathroom. Some items are obvious (long-time annoyances that motivated you to remodel), but you may discover other goals that are equally important. Do not do away with anything yet, even things you think cannot be changed.

Now rank all these goals in order of their importance to you. This list will help you make design decisions and establish budget priorities. It will help you keep perspective if you become frustrated by a stubborn problem or dazzled by a decorator showcase. It will also help you see where you can make trade-offs when faced with limited space, a tight budget, or both. Keep the list handy so you can revise it and refer back to it from time to time. It will change as you absorb new ideas.

RECOGNIZE REALITIES

Up to this point, design possibilities have been wide open. You will have gathered information and set goals, perhaps dealing only with wishes and dreams. Now it's time to identify the practical issues that will set limits on your design. These are the hard realities:
■ Budget
■ Building codes
■ Physical and structural limitations
■ Feasibility of altering plumbing and wiring
■ Amount of work you intend to do yourself.

Do not view these issues as obstacles to creating a wonderful design. View them as opportunities for creative problem solving.

BUDGET CONSIDERATIONS

Generally speaking, a new bathroom costs about as much as a new car. It is a major expenditure, and the amount you spend depends on whether you want an economy pickup truck or a luxury touring sedan. If you select inexpensive materials and do all the work yourself, you can probably remodel your bathroom for less than $5,000. On the other hand, you could spend the same amount on a luxury bathtub!

Before you begin, get some idea of how much you're willing to spend. Investigate all your financing options: savings, a loan secured by a mortgage on your home, or loans secured by other assets.

Establish as firm and realistic a figure as possible. Cost overruns are common in remodeling, so allow for them by establishing a budget that is lower than your reserves.

When you come up with a few preliminary designs, you can hire a contractor to make an estimate or you can make your own (see pages 46-47). The results may send you back to the drawing board, but it is only by moving back and forth between plans and estimates that you will be able to set a budget and stay within its limits.

Your expense is an investment in your home, an investment that can repay you daily in terms of comfort and satisfaction. Its financial payoff is less certain: According to Remodeling magazine, the national average of recouped costs on bathroom remodelings in 1995 was 81 percent, with percentages varying by region from 47 to 144 percent.

DOING IT YOURSELF

Your design may be affected by the amount of planning and construction work you want to do yourself. Assess your own skills and interests as soon as possible.

You may want to work out the design, do the preliminary planning, and manage construction without actually doing any hands-on building. Or you may want to do all demolition and finishing work yourself and hire outside labor for more complicated construction tasks. By knowing what you want to do and being realistic about your skills, you can adjust the design to take advantage of your strengths and avoid costly procedures beyond your abilities.

CODES AND PERMITS

In most places, a remodeling project is subject to certain codes. Depending on the type and scope of the work, these may include zoning, building, plumbing, electrical, mechanical, and possibly energy codes. Visit your local planning or building department to find out what codes pertain and which permits are required. Ask whether you will need prior approval from another agency, such as the sanitation department. If you have a septic system, for example, you may have to upgrade the septic field before you can add a bathroom.

Zoning and design restrictions apply to changes in the exterior of the house. Unless your project involves an addition or exterior alterations, it probably will not be subject to these restrictions.

If there are structural changes, or if the project exceeds a certain amount of money, it will be subject to the building code. In either case, you probably will need a permit. The building code covers structural and safety issues related to construction. For bathroom remodeling, this is likely to include any framing or structural alterations, minimum ceiling heights, clearance below beams, size of doorways, type of window glass, height of steps, and clearances around fixtures.

Your project may be subject to plumbing, electrical, and mechanical codes, although replacing fixtures without moving plumbing or wiring usually does not require a permit. You may be required to bring the plumbing and wiring up to code even if you are not altering any of it. This is a good idea, anyway; it increases safety and enhances value.

It is not necessary to understand every detail of the codes. Just be aware that they will govern some aspects of design and construction. If you hire professional contractors to do the work, they will be responsible for obtaining permits, following codes, and getting all necessary inspections.

STRUCTURAL ISSUES

If you wish to move a wall, add a window, install a skylight, remove the ceiling, or add onto the existing house, you will need to know whether the proposed work is structurally feasible. Some alterations, such as adding a doorway or a window, involve only simple changes in the framing. Other alterations entail major structural changes.

RESEARCH THE PROJECT
continued

To determine whether a change is feasible, you probably will need advice from a builder, designer, or structural engineer to answer these important structural questions:

■ Does it involve walls that support overhead loads?
■ Will a double top plate have to be broken?
■ Must rafters or ceiling joists be altered?
■ Are the floor joists sized properly?
■ Do floor joists run in the right direction?
■ Does the foundation provide adequate support?
■ Is there enough lateral support for large openings?
■ Is there rot or other damage to account for?

The answers will indicate how complex your job will be. But don't immediately rule out changes just because they seem complicated. You may be surprised to discover what is possible.

PLUMBING AND WIRING

Any bathroom remodeling project has the potential for extensive and costly changes in plumbing and wiring. These could involve upgrading the entire plumbing system or adding new circuits to the breaker panel. But plumbing and wiring changes are not always costly. Plastic pipes and fittings have streamlined the modern plumber's work considerably.

Quite often the biggest cost factor is access rather than materials. If you have a clear crawl space or basement below the bathroom and easy access to the attic above, you may be able to make extensive changes at relatively little cost. If you are planning to gut the bathroom, to add insulation, or to resurface all the walls, you may also be able to alter the plumbing and wiring relatively easily. Restricting plumbing fixtures to one wall or to two adjacent walls may make changes simpler, too.

It is impossible to know exactly what is involved until you talk with the person who will be doing the actual work, but you can begin by seeing whether the drainpipes, water supply pipes, and wiring runs are reasonably accessible.

TO DO
1. Investigate all financing options.
2. Assess your do-it-yourself skills, time, and interest.
3. Visit your local building department, usually located in city hall. Find out what local codes pertain to your project and which permits are required.

Bathrooms seem brighter and more spacious when they feature mirrors. This bathroom's broad vanity provides plenty of countertop area and storage space.

DRAW A FLOOR PLAN

Many of your initial ideas may be simple sketches on napkins or paper scraps, but sooner or later you will need an accurate floor plan in order to design your bathroom. For this, you'll need a few inexpensive tools (*see "Tool Box," below*). Most of these you probably have around the house; others can be purchased at any hardware, stationery, or art supply store.

The first step in plan drawing is to sketch a base plan indicating dimensions and permanent fixtures. A comfortable scale for drawing floor plans on graph paper is ½ inch (two ¼-inch squares) to 1 foot.

Begin your base plan by measuring and recording the overall dimensions of the room. Take exact measurements, accurate within ⅛ inch, and record them in feet and inches.

Now add the dimensions of adjacent areas the bathroom might expand into; the length of the wall space between windows, doors, and corners (measure to window jambs and door jambs, not to the edge of trim); the width of the windows and doors (jamb to jamb); and the thickness of the walls.

Draw walls with two parallel lines, the distance between them indicating the thickness of the wall. Shade in the walls to make them easier to see. Indicate windows with a third parallel line between the two wall lines. Show in which direction the doors swing.

DESIGN BY COMPUTER

With the right combination of hardware and software, you can dispense with pencils, tracing paper, and T-squares and develop a detailed plan for your remodeling directly on the computer screen. You can then print out the drawings.

The next step is to measure and indicate the location, width, and depth of each of the fixtures and cabinets that will remain in place. If you have a plastic template in your tool box, it will have sample sizes for common bathroom fixtures.

To complete the base plan, mark the location of the heater, plumbing hookups, electrical outlets, and fan; the location of any steps or other changes in floor height; and the location of overhead features, such as a skylight, low stairs, beams, or duct work. Use broken lines to indicate overhead beams and skylights. Use standard electrical symbols for lights, switches, and outlets.

Photocopy this base plan so you have several copies. During the course of designing your bathroom, you'll want to experiment with location options for all of your fixtures. Having several base plan copies allows convenient experimentation.

TOOL BOX

■ Steel tape measure
■ Ruler or T square
■ Pad of ¼-inch graph paper (4 squares to the inch)
■ Several sharp pencils and erasers
■ Tracing paper
■ Masking tape
■ Clear plastic triangle
■ Compass
■ Plastic template of bathroom elements (optional)

SURVEY YOUR NEEDS

SURVEY: WHAT ARE YOUR WANTS AND NEEDS?

The purpose of this survey is to help you focus on problems and to stimulate creative solutions. The short list following each question is intended as a review of common elements.

GENERAL CONSIDERATIONS

Who uses the bathroom? When? Do certain members of the household use it at the same time? Is it used by anyone who has special needs, such as a youngster or a disabled person? Will there be changes in the family in the near future? Do visitors use this bathroom? Overnight guests? Is the bathroom used for other activities, such as laundry? Can these activities be done elsewhere? Have you any long-range plans for remodeling your home? Do they include the addition of another bathroom?

☐ Number of users
☐ Ages of users
☐ Special needs of users
☐ Additional room uses
☐ Future room needs
☐ Privacy considerations

OVERALL DESIGN

What are your first impressions upon entering the bathroom? Do you like the way it looks? What do you like and dislike about it? Is it too bright? Too dark? Too small? Too sterile? Too boring? Cold? Garish? Cramped? Old-fashioned? Somber? Spacious? As you list the characteristics you like and dislike, note the particular elements—color, light, style—that contribute to the atmosphere you want.

☐ Overall impression
☐ Current style
☐ Style of adjoining rooms
☐ Features to retain
☐ Problem features to eliminate

SPACE, TRAFFIC, LAYOUT

Is there enough space in the bathroom? If not, why not? Are too many people using a limited number of fixtures? Are secondary activities (exercise, laundry, pet care) taking up valuable space? Is there enough counter space? Enough mirror area? Enough privacy? Does the door swing into the room and take up useful space? Are there any wasted areas? Which fixture is used most frequently? (It's usually the sink.) Is it easy to get to? Is there more than one entrance to the bathroom? If so, is it necessary? Is there space next to the bathroom for expansion—an extra closet, a dead-end hallway, or an extra large bedroom? Are dressing areas close to the bathroom? Are laundry facilities convenient?

☐ Current fixtures
☐ Desired fixtures
☐ Can space be expanded?
☐ Door swing direction
☐ Minimum clearances

STORAGE

Is there enough storage space? Is it efficient? Are there items you don't need to store in the bathroom? Are there items you'd like to store in the bathroom but don't have room? Is the room messy because there is no organized storage space for towels, toothbrushes, etc.? Do you prefer open storage or closed? Would you rather display towels or keep them hidden?

☐ Towel storage
☐ Linen storage
☐ Bulk paper product storage
☐ Appliance storage
☐ Safe medicine storage
☐ Safe cleaning product storage
☐ Storage accessibility

HEATING

Is the bathroom warm enough? Too warm? What is the heat source? Can it be moved or changed, if necessary? What changes would you favor?

☐ Type of heat
☐ Type of ventilation
☐ Noise considerations

FINISH SURFACES

What are the wall, ceiling, and floor coverings? What do you like and dislike about these materials? Are they easy or hard to keep clean? Have they chipped, peeled, mildewed, cracked, or deteriorated? Are colors satisfactory? Have the surfaces worn well? Would you want to use these same materials again?

☐ Wall finishes
☐ Floor finishes
☐ Ceiling finishes
☐ Shower surround
☐ Bathtub surround
☐ Are finishes sound?
☐ Are colors compatible?

FIXTURES AND FITTINGS

In bathrooms, "fixtures" refers to the sink, toilet, tub, shower, and bidet. The word "fittings" refers to faucets, handles, exposed pipes, and similar hardware. What do you like and dislike about each fixture and fitting? Do they look dated? Are they easy to use? Are the colors satisfactory? Are they difficult to clean? Would you prefer a single-control faucet where you now have two-handled faucets? Would you prefer two faucets where you now have one? Do you wish to keep any fixtures or fittings? If you wish to replace any, do you have a particular replacement in mind?

- ☐ Sink style
- ☐ Faucet style
- ☐ Shower style
- ☐ Shower head style
- ☐ Bathtub style
- ☐ Toilet style
- ☐ Are fixtures sound?
- ☐ Are fittings sound?

ACCESSORIES AND HARDWARE

Small details often make or break a design. Are there any items you don't have that you want? Are there any items that you have and don't use? Are your present accessories conveniently located? Do you like the colors, materials, and design?

- ☐ Mirror
- ☐ Laundry hamper
- ☐ Towel bars
- ☐ Clothes hooks
- ☐ Toothbrush holder
- ☐ Toilet paper holder
- ☐ Door handles
- ☐ Drawer pulls
- ☐ Book or magazine rack
- ☐ Wastebasket
- ☐ Soap dishes
- ☐ Rug

LIGHTING AND ELECTRICAL OUTLETS

Are there any sources of natural light? If so, during what part of the day is the room brightest? In what direction does the window face? Is there wall space where a window would be appropriate? Is there enough privacy? Is there enough artificial light? Is it incandescent or fluorescent? Is the light too harsh or too soft? Does it shine where you need it the most? Do you like the lighting fixtures? Are there enough electrical outlets? Where are they located? Do you need additional outlets for hair dryers, curling irons, and electric razors? Could outlets be placed more conveniently? Are existing outlets designated GFCI (ground fault circuit interrupter) as is required in bathrooms? What electrical fixtures (fan, heater, ventilator, heat lamp) are permanently installed? Are you satisfied with their locations? If not, what changes would you suggest?

- ☐ Number of windows
- ☐ Window sizes
- ☐ Available views
- ☐ Skylight possibilities
- ☐ Decorative light fixtures
- ☐ Additional light sources
- ☐ Number of electrical outlets
- ☐ Outlet positions
- ☐ Currently installed appliances
- ☐ Desired installed appliances
- ☐ Small appliances used regularly
- ☐ Laundry facilities

SPECIAL NEEDS

Are there people in your household who have or who soon may have special needs? Children? Elderly adults? Someone who is disabled? Someone who is exceptionally tall or short? Is the toilet at a comfortable height? Are there grab bars near the toilet, tub, shower? Can children be bathed without discomfort to the person who is doing the bathing? Is the door wide enough for a wheelchair? Can children reach the faucets? Is the sink at the right height for everyone in the household? Is there provision for sitting in the shower?

- ☐ Installed grab bars
- ☐ Sink height and position
- ☐ Toilet style and type
- ☐ Special bathing needs
- ☐ Bathtub height
- ☐ Shower head height
- ☐ Door width for special access
- ☐ Check minimum clearances

LUXURIES

Are there any luxury fixtures in or adjacent to the bathroom, such as a whirlpool bath, steam room, hot tub, or sauna? Would you like to have any of these? Where would you put them? Will the existing plumbing and electrical capacity handle these luxuries?

- ☐ Whirlpool bath
- ☐ Sauna
- ☐ Steam room
- ☐ Intercom
- ☐ Telephone
- ☐ Television with remote control
- ☐ Radio or stereo with speakers
- ☐ Pet needs
- ☐ Gas fireplace

LAYOUT GUIDELINES

The trick to good powder rooms and three-quarter baths is to make them compact but not crowded. They are often used by guests so finishes tend to be elegant.

Size can vary from a tiny half bath tucked away in a closet to a grand bathing suite the size of a common living room. Such variations in scale, as well as in shape and function, create almost endless possibilities when it comes to layouts.

These layouts illustrate how various types of bathrooms can be arranged in rooms of different sizes and shapes. Though none may suit your needs exactly, they show how fixtures can be arranged in a given space.

THREE-QUARTER

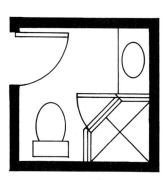
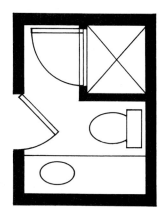

POWDER ROOM

POWDER ROOM

A powder room (or half bath) consists of a toilet and sink, located near areas where visitors gather. They tend to be small and are frequented by guests, so powder rooms often are finished with finer materials than those used in larger baths.

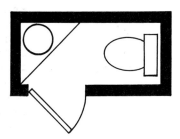

THREE-QUARTER

A shower stall instead of a bathtub, plus a toilet and sink, make up a three-quarter bath. These can be squeezed into spaces as small as 6×6 feet and are a good backup to the main family bath. They are suitable bathrooms for older children and overnight guests.

FAMILY

The layout of the family bathroom offers the greatest variety of options. This room must meet the needs of every member of the household, and sometimes these needs conflict. The need for privacy may clash with the need for several people to use the bathroom at once, or the need to store personal items in the bathroom may not mesh

FAMILY

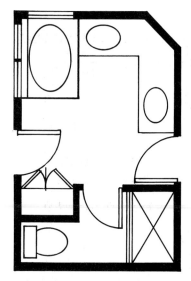
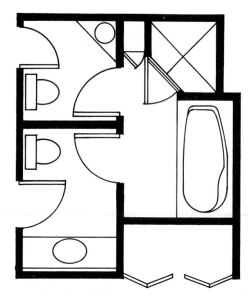
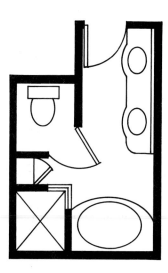

with the need to make it available to guests. If the present bathroom is large enough, you may be able to solve the privacy problem by transforming part of it into a separate half bath or by compartmentalizing it so that several people can use the room simultaneously.

MULTIPLE-ENTRY

A bathroom with more than one entrance (from a hallway and a bedroom, for example) allows for greater access—but at a price. Although the doorway itself takes up relatively little space, each entrance becomes a major element in the design when you consider the space required for the door swing and access to the door. Multiple entrances compound the problem by creating traffic corridors that divide and shrink usable space. If you are unable to eliminate one of the doorways, consider moving it to improve traffic flow and free up space. You might also consider installing pocket doors, which require less space than standard ones.

MASTER

Master bathrooms are private retreats that lend themselves to luxurious amenities and creative planning. Some are modest baths placed next to the bedroom for convenience. Others are large suites that may include a dressing room, closets, a sitting area, and an exercise area.

A master suite may include complete his-and-hers bathrooms. If this is what you are considering, think about dividing the bathing fixtures between the two areas. Consider, for example, a large shower and no bathtub in one

MULTIPLE ENTRY

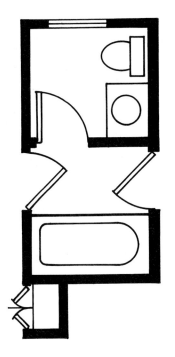

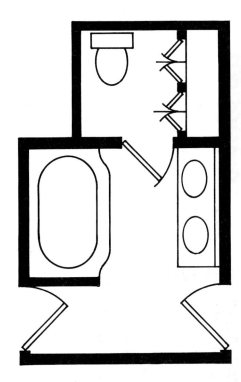

bathroom and a whirlpool tub without a shower in the other.

OPEN-STYLE

An open bathroom is a highly personal space that forms part of a larger bedroom or suite. The centerpiece is usually a large soaking tub; the toilet, bidet, and shower are compartmentalized. This type of bathroom takes special planning to ensure that the various spaces relate well to one another, as well as to the larger room.

Storage and occupancy lead concerns for family baths. Some master baths double as dressing rooms, so consider the relationship between the bath and closets.

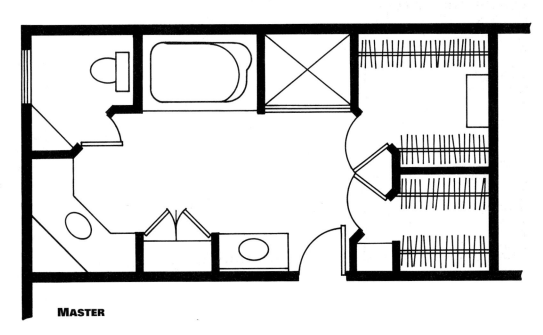

MASTER

ENLARGING THE SPACE

If the existing space is simply too small, now is the time to look for ways to expand. First see if anything can be moved out of the bathroom to create more space. If you want two sinks, consider installing one in an adjacent bedroom. Place it on the common wall between the bedroom and the bathroom to make the plumbing easier. If a large storage unit or cabinet takes up valuable space, consider other storage options. Perhaps you could build shelves or soffit cabinets near the ceiling, install a high cabinet above the toilet, or recess narrow shelves into a wall.

ANNEXING: You may be able to annex space for the bathroom from adjacent areas. Are there closets, dead-end hallways, unused rooms, or storage areas that the bathroom could expand into? If the bathroom has two or more entrances, could one be closed off? Does the bathroom have an entry area that

PLUMBING TIPS

The wall containing the plumbing pipes is called a "wet wall." The fewer wet walls you have, the less costly your plumbing will be. Though it's cheapest to have only one wet wall, it is also the most limiting design-wise.

Adding or moving bathroom fixtures can be expensive, even if you're only moving them a few feet. That's why it's important to take maximum advantage of your present plumbing configuration—both the water supply lines and the drainage, waste, and vent lines.

Because each new or moved bathroom fixture must connect with a main soil stack, you must know the locations of your main vents, then determine a route for attaching new vent lines to them. Building codes are very specific about size and general conformation of drainage, waste, and vent lines. Unless you're an accomplished do-it-yourselfer, it's best to leave major plumbing jobs to a professional.

Also think about placement of fixtures. The sink, for example, should be positioned closest to the door because it's usually the last stop in the routine. Having to squeeze by other fixtures on your way in and out of the door can be inconvenient.

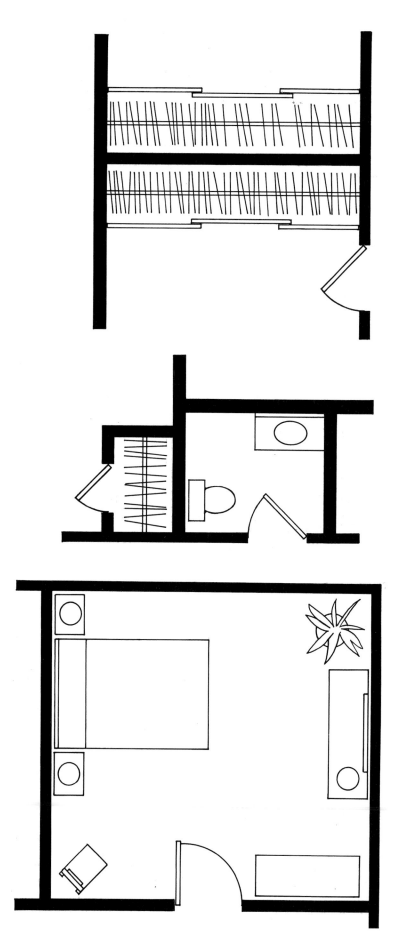

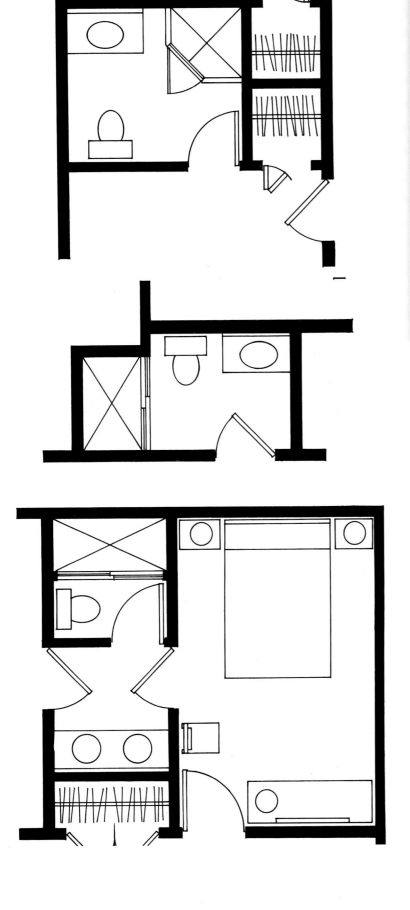

could be better used by moving the door closer to the hallway? Are there places for recessed storage shelves within the wall cavities, or places where cabinets or shelves could extend through the wall into an adjacent room?

DISPLACING: A more drastic solution is to carve a completely new bathroom out of some other space in the house. Perhaps there is an underutilized office or den, or a bedroom that is far too large. The old bathroom could be used as a powder room, or the two spaces could be switched so that the old bathroom becomes a new, small den. Consider this solution if you are already planning to gut the old bathroom and completely remodel it.

If budget and space allow, you can always expand the bathroom outward. Some additions are modest bump-outs that cantilever beyond the existing foundation without requiring a new foundation. Others are major annexes that include a complete bathing suite. One popular type of bathroom addition is a prefabricated sun space, often enclosing a luxury whirlpool spa.

Closets and guest rooms are likely sources of space for adding or expanding a bath.

DESIGN: PRACTICALITY WITH STYLE

There are no absolutes in good bathroom design. There are only pragmatic issues and aesthetic issues. It all boils down to one question: Is the design optimally functional and do you like the way it looks?

Function is the basic building block of the design. It defines how well the bathroom meets practical needs and determines such factors as layout, storage, and location of fixtures.

Some of the design is generated by the space itself. A good design highlights the best features of the room and plays down the worst. On the one hand, if the room is large and light and has an enormous panoramic view, a good design will focus on the window. On the other hand, if the window opens on a dusty air shaft, it makes sense to obscure the view (but not the light or ventilation).

Beyond these practical considerations is the aesthetic impact of the room, which can range from animated, dramatic, and spectacular to understated, peaceful, and serene. Your choices here are a matter of personal taste and style. Design is a very individual preference.

There is no right or wrong style. However, it is important to know what your style is and how various elements contribute or detract from it. Even when you are sketching basic floor plans—putting the tub here or the sink there—your design will go much more smoothly if you have a clear idea of the look and tone you're trying to achieve.

DESIGN PRINCIPLES

How can you tie together all the elements in your bathroom to create the overall look you want to achieve? The secret is to follow the basic principles of good design—line, form, scale, pattern, texture, and color.

LINE: Edges, corners, and decorative features of all the elements in the room create an abundance of lines. The bathroom will feel more integrated and harmonious if these elements align as much as possible. For instance, the top of a doorway creates a horizontal line. If there is a window or a tall cabinet in the room, the design will be smoother if the top edge lines up with the top of the door molding. When it is impossible to position elements so that the edges are aligned, you can still create a unified feeling by introducing a line of tile or a strip of molding to coordinate the elements.

FORM: Continuity in form also lends harmony to a design. Look at the shapes of the doors, windows, shower stall, bathtub, vanity, and cabinets. Do they repeat a similar form or do they clash? Is there one unique shape—a curved window or an archway, for example? If so, you may want to repeat this shape elsewhere.

SCALE: Properly scaled spaces are neither too large nor too small for the people who use them. When considering the proper scale for the bathroom, look at the size of the room and the sizes of the fixtures and finishes. If the room feels cramped, try using fixtures that are smaller than standard, small tiles, and a delicately patterned curtain fabric. If the room feels large or has a large window that expands the vista, think big.

PATTERN: Defined as "repeated shapes," pattern also is the ordered regularity of the design elements. In most bathrooms, the goal is to strike a balance between too much of the same pattern and too many different ones. One approach is to reduce pattern to a bare minimum or to use a few homogeneous, fine-patterned materials. The other approach is to introduce materials with random patterns—such as flat-grained wood cabinets, wall coverings with floral designs, stacks of towels, plants—to break up monotony.

TEXTURE: Most bathroom textures—all visual and tactile surfaces—are smooth for durability and easy cleaning, but even smooth surfaces can vary. Consider the differences to the touch among polished wood, glazed tile, porcelain, and glass. Think about texture when you choose all of your materials. Do you want your bathroom to feel sleek and shiny? Or do you prefer soft, natural finishes?

COLOR: Color can transform space and give it much of its character. Consider the physical effects colors produce. Reds, oranges, and yellows are warm. Blues, greens, and violets are cool. You also can use color to alter the spatial characteristics of the room. If the bathroom is small, use light colors to make it feel more spacious. If the ceiling is low, a light color will cause it to recede. If it is high and makes the bathroom feel too formal, use dark colors on the floor and countertops to create a more intimate feeling. Make a long, narrow bathroom feel wider by using light colors on the long walls and a dark color on the short end wall. Use intense colors to emphasize features, and pale colors to play them down.

REFINING THE FLOOR PLAN

Once you have surveyed the present bathroom, gathered ideas for the new design, chosen an overall style, and drawn a sketch of the base plan, you will be bursting with ideas. Now you will want to make some sketches to begin designing your new room.

Begin by drawing a few preliminary floor plans and experimenting with different layouts. Use the base floor plan of the existing bathroom, drawn to scale, as a start. Simply lay a sheet of tracing paper over it and sketch your new ideas on that. Make as many tracings as you need. Or make several photocopies of the existing floor plan and sketch your ideas directly onto those. You can use these photocopies throughout the design process.

First position the major fixtures—toilet, bathtub, shower. Try keeping them where they are. If this doesn't work or if you plan to use different fixtures, start from scratch. If possible, find out exactly where you can rough in new drainpipes and vent pipes for the tub,

toilet, and shower. Concentrate on these locations for the major fixtures as you try new layouts. Don't worry about extending the water supply pipes; they can be run almost anywhere the drainpipes can go.

To avoid having to sketch a new floor plan each time you try out a new idea, draw templates of the main elements to scale and cut them out. Then you can simply move them around on an open floor plan until you find a layout that works. Include the main plumbing fixtures (toilet, bathtub, shower, sink, and any storage units you will be using). Refer to the manufacturer's specifications for exact dimensions.

Give yourself several weeks to complete this process. Don't commit to one particular layout until you have experimented with all possibilities. Take some chances. Have fun. The important thing is to define the problems, then be open to solutions sparked by imaginative thinking but grounded in reality.

This sleek, functional bath is divided into three sections— a grooming area with double pedestal sinks, a private toilet compartment, and a shower with overhead skylight.

REFINING THE DESIGN

Design is a give-and-take process. It requires a balance of specific details with overall style. Best advice: Try to give the same attention to small details as you give to major elements. Well-defined details can make the difference between a satisfactory bathroom and a stunningly beautiful one.

This chapter will help you refine your preliminary layout. Be prepared to change the layout as new ideas occur to you.

Though it's useful to start with major elements, it's not essential because all design elements are related. All details, however, must be carefully thought out in the planning stage.

Don't overlook safety. The bathroom is the site of more falls in the home than any other room. Before beginning construction, be certain the layout and design details will render a safe bathroom.

Shiny green ceramic tile, light wood tones, and sponged walls give this bathroom an Italian flair.

PLUMBING FIXTURES

Though all fixtures in this old-fashioned bath share a common plumbing wall, an interior partition creates a private compartment for the toilet.

As you plan each plumbing fixture, consider location, size, type, style, color, material, special features, convenience, and plumbing access.

Consider, too, whether the fixtures should function as a coordinated ensemble or as individual pieces. Whatever your preference, this section will help you examine factors related to each fixture.

CHOOSING COLOR

When choosing color for any bathroom fixture, consider the overall scheme as well as cost. White is generally the least expensive.

If you want the fixture to be subdued and unobtrusive, choose a neutral color matching the floor or surrounding walls. If you want to emphasize the fixture's lines, choose white, light gray, or a pastel. For a bold statement, choose a bright color.

■ White is classic and never goes out of date.
■ Bone and almond suggest warmth.
■ Dark colors (such as navy blue or deep raspberry, and especially black) are very sensual but are harder to maintain.
■ Bright red or yellow creates a bold accent.
■ Grays and pastels suggest refined elegance.
■ Blues, greens, and marine colors are always appropriate in a home near a body of water.

DESIGN TIP

If the toilet is next to the vanity, consider extending the countertop in a graceful curve over the tank part of the toilet to maximize space. This is called a "banjo countertop."

TOILET

Depending on the floor plan, the toilet can be placed along a wall, in a shallow alcove, or in a compartment of its own. Most toilets are 20 to 24 inches wide and extend approximately 27 inches from the wall if they have a conventional rounded bowl, and 30 inches if they have an elongated bowl. Height depends on whether the tank is separate or is incorporated into a low-profile, one-piece design. One-piece toilets are 19-20 inches high; two-piece toilets are 26-28 inches high.

CONSIDER FUNCTION: By law, toilets manufactured since January 1, 1994, may use no more than 1.6 gallons of water per flush. Some use even less. Old toilets (though they cost less) use 3.5 or more gallons of water per flush. To produce a sanitary flush, low-flow toilets generate greater water velocity.

Noise is another consideration. Some toilets flush more quietly than others. Hard surfaces (such as tile or marble) amplify any sound within the bathroom, whereas plastic drainpipes and unsecured water pipes amplify the sound of water and carry it throughout the house.

Wall-mounted models free up floor space for easier cleaning and a less cluttered look. Like conventional toilets with a rear outlet, they solve the problem of roughing in a new toilet drain in a bathroom with a concrete slab floor.

Other options include:
- Insulating liners that prevent condensation
- Elongated bowls
- Extra high models, with a rim 18 inches above the floor instead of 15 inches
- Reinforced seat with supporting arms
- Corner toilets to maximize floor space

STYLE OPTIONS

A prominently located toilet commands as much attention as a large sculpture, so consider carefully how it fits into the design.

The main style options are size, shape, and color. A low, one-piece toilet will not be as prominent as a two-piece toilet. For that reason, it can fit into a wider range of design schemes. A two-piece, or tank, toilet has greater bulk, which can be a benefit in some designs and a distraction in others.

Shape and styling give the fixture grace and form. Some toilets have strong angles and geometric shapes. Others have soft, flowing lines. Some shapes and styles evoke a specific period. Compare models to see which one blends best with your design scheme.

Matching seats are available for most toilets, but you can select a different seat to create a contrast or to unify the toilet with other elements in the room—a wood seat to match the vanity, for example.

PLUMBING CONSIDERATIONS

When selecting a toilet, verify the rough-in dimensions for the drain and the water supply valve. For most toilets the floor drain is centered 12 inches out from the finish wall. When verifying the location of the supply valve, check the measurements with the actual toilet or a showroom model. Manufacturers sometimes specify generic measurements, and you can modify them so that the supply tube rises gracefully toward the tank inlet without any unnecessary loops or kinks.

THE BIDET

Although bidets are not used as widely in the United States as they are in Europe, they are gaining popularity. The fixture works like a sink and is designed for cleansing the perineal region. It can be used by any member of the family. It can be filled with water from the faucet spout, but modern bidets also provide a flow of water around the rim to rinse it. Some offer the option of a continuous stream of water ascending from the center of the bowl.

For convenience, locate the bidet close to the toilet. If the two fixtures are installed side by side, leave at least 15 inches between them. Check local codes to determine the required minimum clearance. Expect the fixture to take up at least 3 square feet of floor space.

Unlike a toilet, a bidet must be plumbed with both hot and cold water, as well as a drain. Most plumbing codes also require a vacuum breaker in the water supply piping if there are any water inlets below the rim of the bidet.

PLUMBING FIXTURES
continued

BATHTUB

Few things in a house are more permanent than the bathtub. Because it can't be easily moved or replaced, choose your tub with care. You'll be living with it for a long time.

Before choosing a new tub, consider keeping the old one. An enameled cast-iron bathtub in good condition is worth keeping if you can renew it. By changing the faucet, retiling the tub enclosure (or refinishing it with marble or solid-surface material), and adding new doors or a stylish curtain, you can make an old fixture look as handsome as a new one. Even a rusted, worn cast-iron tub can be professionally refinished, in place, with a new surface that will last for years.

LOCATION: Consider the practical issues of access and plumbing. The tub should be convenient but should not impede the flow of traffic. It should be easy to get into and out of. If you are locating the faucet and spout on an exterior wall, make sure local plumbing codes allow it—some codes prohibit pipes in exterior walls for reasons of energy conservation or accessibility.

A small door or removable panel should be included on the end wall to provide access to drainpipes and overflow pipes. The tub or shower valve can usually be reached through the front cover plate. If you want to locate the tub where it is impossible to place a new drain under the floor, you can raise the tub on a platform or get a tub with a raised bottom. The drainpipe and P-trap can be installed above floor level in an adjacent wall.

Other factors to consider are convenience to dressing areas and structural support. Most residential floors are designed to carry 40 pounds per square foot. A 3×6-foot tub filled with 60 gallons of water and containing two adults will produce a total load of about 53 pounds per square foot. A cast-iron tub weighs much more, and some tubs hold more water. Get professional advice about the need to reinforce the floor if you plan to install a large bathtub.

SIZE AND TYPE: Although bathtubs are available in many sizes and shapes, the standard tub is 5 feet long, 30 inches wide, and 14–16 inches high. It has a finish skirt on only one side and is meant to be installed between two walls. It comes with the drain on the left or right. Tubs 4½-feet and 5½-feet long are also available in standard width.

Bathtubs made of new lightweight materials—acrylics reinforced with fiberglass—are available in a variety of shapes and sizes. Some have skirts, but most have unfinished sides and are intended for platform installation. Typical outside dimensions are approximately 5 feet long by 36, 40, 42, 44, or 48 inches wide; 5 ½ feet long by 30 or 36 inches wide; and 6 feet long by 33, 36, 42, 48, 56, or 60 inches wide. Get exact dimensions from the supplier or from the manufacturer's specifications.

Do not rely on the outside dimensions of bathtubs for comparing sizes. The interior bathing space is what counts. If possible, compare bathtubs by sitting in them, especially if more than one person will be using the tub.

Corner tubs can be installed in spaces too small for a standard tub. The bathing area, which is positioned diagonally, is standard size, and the tub feels less cramped than a standard tub because there is a wide shelf in the corner. Traditional cast-iron corner tubs measure 4 feet or less along each side. In acrylic models, each side usually measures 48 to 55 inches.

If you like the charm of an old-fashioned claw-foot tub, you can buy a modern replica or have an old tub refinished. Faucets and fittings for an old tub may be found through renovator supply catalogs or specialty outlets.

MATERIALS: Enameled cast-iron bathtubs are the most durable and come in a wide array of colors. They feel solid, retain heat well, cushion sounds, and resist stains. They are also heavy; floors may require structural reinforcement to take the larger sizes.
■ Enameled steel tubs are less expensive than cast-iron ones, but they chip easily, can sound tinny, and come in a limited choice of colors.
■ Acrylic and fiberglass tubs offer the widest choice of sizes and shapes. They are lightweight and hold heat better than tubs made of other materials. They come in deep and high-gloss colors as well as in standard colors and white. They are easily drilled for custom faucet installations. The quality and durability of the finish have improved, and with proper care the new tubs will resist stains and scratches fairly well.
■ Cast polymer tubs offer many of these same features.
■ Real marble (for the high-end market) is covered with clear acrylic for durability.
■ A custom-made ceramic tile tub looks magnificent, but the flat planes and square edges characteristic of most tiling render them uncomfortable for long, relaxing baths. This problem can be solved by using small mosaic tiles applied over curved surfaces to create a more contoured, comfortable shape.

WHIRLPOOLS

In a whirlpool system, water is pumped from the tub, mixed with air, and forced back into the tub through jets. This system is intended more for massaging than for cleansing, so a separate shower is convenient for washing up before or after the soak. Unlike a spa, which has a filtering and heating system, a whirlpool bath is drained after each use.

Whirlpool tubs are available in many sizes. If you enjoy lingering baths and you have space, a roomy tub can be a focal point of your new bathroom and a highlight of your day. You will have a choice of jets—either a few large jets producing a soft, soothing bath or several small, high-pressure jets producing a forceful current for a stimulating massage. The motor is mounted at one end of the tub and must be accessible for servicing.

Plan an access door, either at the end of the tub or in the side, as specified by the manufacturer. The whirlpool should have a safety switch for turning it on and off while you are in the tub. Also consider whether the hot-water system has the capacity to fill the tub quickly. A 50-gallon hot-water tank is usually adequate, but check with a plumber or the whirlpool supplier.

Be sure you are getting a whirlpool for the right reasons. It may be that what you want is a large, comfortable tub for long, hot baths and not necessarily the massage action. If so, you can get a large soaking tub without the expensive whirlpool feature.

TUB OPTIONS

- Nonskid bottom
- Grab bars
- Pillows
- Built-in sound system
- Heaters to keep water hot
- Integral sides eliminating the need for a waterproof enclosure

A platform tub can be enclosed in any style from rustic to sleek. In addition to its distinctive built-in look, this design has plenty of surface area around the tub for bathing supplies.

PLUMBING FIXTURES
continued

SHOWER

Having a shower separate from the tub is a high priority in many bathrooms. Master bathrooms often have both a luxury tub and a walk-in shower. Some even have separate his-and-hers showers.

If space is tight, finding room for a shower can be a problem. Perhaps you can annex space from an adjacent closet, hallway, or bedroom. If there is not enough space for both a shower and a tub, choose either a combination tub/shower or do without a tub.

The smallest practical size for a shower stall is 34 inches square on the inside dimension. For more comfort and elbow room, a 36-inch square is better.

LOCATION: A shower stall can go anywhere in the bathroom as long as you maintain sufficient clearance in front of the door. When choosing a location, consider natural light, ventilation, access to towels, and access to a clear area for toweling off. Consider, too, how easy it will be for someone to use the rest of the bathroom while the shower is occupied.

TYPES: There are three types of showers:
■ PREFABRICATED UNITS: Installed in much the same way as other plumbing fixtures, these come in a variety of shapes, sizes, and colors. Most are square or rectangular, with one open side for a doorway or two open sides, one to take a glass panel and one for a doorway. Options include:
• Corner units with a diagonal front.
• No-threshold models for wheelchair use.
• Luxury units that convert into steam rooms.

Sizes range from 32 inch squares (not large enough to meet some local codes) to 36×48 inch rectangles. The most common material is fiberglass with a finish surface of acrylic or other plastic. All of these finishes require nonabrasive cleaners. Walls of the unit must be attached to rigid framing. No tiling is required. Some units have ceilings. Some have doors, but for most the door must be purchased separately. Some have molded seats, soap dishes, and ledges.

Prefab showers are quite easy to install. Usually, the most difficult problem is getting them into the bathroom because they are larger than a standard doorway. Some models come in two or more sections that can be assembled in place.

DESIGN TIP

To make a small bathroom feel less closed in, use a shower curtain rather than a glass door. Or install a large mirror.

■ PREFABRICATED SHOWER PANS: Molded from plastic, terrazzo, or similar chipped stone, this type enables you to choose walls of any material without having to order a custom waterproof shower pan. They can be used with prefabricated shower surrounds or custom materials, such as tile, marble, or solid surface slabs. The stone pans look and feel more substantial than most plastic or fiberglass pans. Options include:
• Range of colors
• Skid-resistant floors (which can be difficult to clean)
• Wide range of sizes
■ CUSTOMMADE SHOWER STALLS: For the most flexibility, custom showers can be designed to match your space, your bathing needs, and your creative imagination. Some are small rooms with multiple shower heads and may double as steam rooms. Others are open stalls with low walls making them feel more a part of the surrounding room. Some have windows with panoramic vistas. Some are circular, like seashells. Vaulted ceilings and skylights may complete a dramatic effect.

Walls can be made of tile, marble, solid surface material, cast polymer, tempered glass, glass block, or other materials that are waterproof and easily maintained. The floor pan must be installed properly to prevent leaking. This usually is best achieved by a professional plumber or tile setter.

Whatever type of stall you choose, you have design flexibility regarding wall and ceiling height. If you prefer maximum closure, consider a lower ceiling, such as 7 feet. Run the tile up to and across the ceiling to control moisture problems. If you like a more open feeling, build the enclosure walls only $6\frac{1}{2}$ feet high with 18 inches of space above them.

DOORS AND SIDE PANELS: Prefabricated shower doors are available in many styles and configurations. For recessed stalls, you will need only a door, with jambs and hardware for mounting it in the opening. For stalls with one or more open sides, you can order fixed, matching panels. These panels must be made of tempered glass, safety glass, wire glass, or plastic. You have a choice of clear, etched, or smoked glass. The metal edge, or frame, which holds the door and panels can be finished in chrome, brass, brushed gold, bronze, white, black, or a number of decorator colors. Frameless doors also are available.

Some doors are hinged along the edge. Others have pivots attached to the top and bottom to minimize the arc of the door swing and to provide a tighter seal. Sliding doors are available for wide openings. Most door and side panel assemblies are approximately 70 inches high.

FAUCET AND SHOWER HEAD

Selecting a faucet and a showerhead is no longer a simple matter of choosing between chrome and brass finishes. You have a variety to options to consider. For instance, in selecting the handle action, you have a choice between two separate handles and a single handle. In a single handle, you can choose a knob, a lever, or a combination of both. Visit a showroom where you can test different models to compare the action, as well as the styling.

You have functional choices, also. Many shower faucets include an anti-scald feature, which keeps water at an even temperature when someone runs water elsewhere in the house. This is mandated by many local codes for new installations. Some faucets have digital readouts to tell you the water temperature.

When selecting a faucet, price is often a good indicator of quality. A high quality

faucet carries a warranty and is made from heavy brass parts that are easy to replace.

Showerheads offer even more options:
■ Watersaving features
■ Massage sprays
■ Flexible tubing for handheld or stationary operation
■ A wall bar for adjusting the height of the showerhead
■ Multiple heads for body spraying
■ A wide range of styles and finishes

"Beam me up, Scotty"? Modern materials lend a space-age look to this shower stall, which resembles a teleportation chamber in a sci-fi flick. Today's showers can be good, clean fun.

PLUMBING FIXTURES
continued

SINK

Although it's the smallest of the plumbing fixtures, the sink (or lavatory) is used most often. Because it's usually used just before anyone leaves the bathroom, it should be located near the door.

Freestanding sinks expose more of the floor and wall areas, making the room feel larger. They are sculptural objects, with graceful lines and contoured surfaces. Drawbacks include exposed plumbing and lack of countertop and storage space.

Wall-hung sinks squeeze into small spaces and make a room feel larger because they expose the floor. They also lack counter space and storage room, but wall-hung sinks can accommodate wheelchairs.

Countertop installation has the advantage of providing a convenient work surface, and it makes the sink blend into the furnishings. Because the sink usually includes a vanity, it provides storage and conceals plumbing. The main drawbacks are the potential for clutter and loss of floor space.

LOCATION AND NUMBER: There are several satisfactory ways to fit two sinks into a bathroom. One is to use a long or L-shaped counter. If the sinks are side by side, allow at least 30 inches of counter for each (a total of 5 feet). Another option is to separate the sinks, perhaps placing them back to back in a peninsula or island configuration. They also might be placed on adjacent walls. Allow at least 3 feet of maneuvering space in front of each sink. Another option is to move one sink into the dressing area or a separate compartment outside the main bathroom to provide privacy in both spaces.

Other factors affecting location are ease of access from the bathroom entry; natural light from a window or skylight; and sufficient space for such amenities.

SIZE AND SHAPE: Countertop sinks can be round, oval, rectangular, hexagonal, or customized in any shape. Round basins are usually 18–19 inches in diameter. Oval basins are 17–20 inches wide and 14–17 inches deep (front to back). Most rectangular basins are 20–22 inches wide and 17–19 inches deep, but they can be as wide as 28 inches or as small as 11×11 inches. Hexagons are 20–22 inches wide, 16–19 inches deep.

Wall-mounted sinks are rectangular. Most models are 19–20 inches wide and 17–18 inches deep. Smaller models are typically 16 inches wide and 12 inches deep.

Pedestal sinks are 20–28 inches wide, 16–21 inches deep, and 30–32 inches high.

Besides size and shape, consider the placement of holes for the faucet.

MATERIAL DIFFERENCES: The function may not change, but the sink's appearance, durability, and style are affected by the material from which it is made. Among the most popular choices:

■ VITREOUS CHINA SINKS, the most common choice, are durable, easy to clean, and beautiful, but they can crack or chip if treated roughly.

■ ENAMELED CAST-IRON SINKS are easy to clean and more durable than vitreous china but not as smooth. They are heavy and need support.

■ POTTERY SINKS are made in limited production, typically in earth colors, and have the feeling of custom-made, one-of-a-kind pieces. The durability and surface smoothness of these sinks depends on the glaze.

■ CAST POLYMER SINKS are molded into countertops of the same material. They may have a gelcoat or a clear finish that may eventually wear away.

■ SIMULATED MARBLE AND OTHER SOLID-SURFACE MATERIALS are handsome, durable, and available in several colors and styles, including faux granite. They may chip when struck by a heavy object, and abrasive cleaners spoil the finish.

A massive pedestal sink, gleaming in sunlight streaming through a bathroom window, takes on a sculptural quality in this handsomely renovated bath.

TO DO

As soon as you have selected a sink, use the manufacturer's specifications to revise your rough plan.

■ ENAMELED PRESSED STEEL, the least expensive type of sink, is lightweight, fairly durable, and easy to clean.

■ COMPOSITE MATERIALS, such as epoxy and compressed quartz, are lightweight and available in bold, dramatic colors.

FAUCETS

Think of faucets as jewelry for the fixtures. It is not uncommon to spend more money on the faucet than on the fixture itself. If you're investing in quality, don't settle for cheap faucets.

TYPES: Make sure the faucet set is the proper size and design to fit your sink. Most sinks come with holes drilled in their rims to accommodate standard faucets and plumbing. There are three basic types of faucets:

■ SINGLE CONTROL FAUCETS have one spout for both hot and cold water.

■ CENTER-SET FAUCETS, with spout and handles in one unit, have single or dual controls. Most are designed for a three-hole basin, with the outside holes spaced 4 inches from center to center. Some have a single-post design that requires only one hole.

■ SPREAD-FIT FAUCETS separate spout and handles. The connection between them is concealed below the deck. They can be adapted to fit holes spaced 4–16 inches apart. They can be individualized even more if they are mounted in a countertop next to the sink. For example, the spout could be placed at a rear corner and the handles off to the side. This is handy for tight installations where there is no room for a full faucet at the back of the basin.

FINISH AND STYLE: Faucet bodies are usually of brass and covered with a finish. The traditional finish is chrome, which is easy to maintain and lasts for years. Unplated brass also is popular in bronze, antique matte, or highly polished finishes. Brass tends to tarnish easily, so various protective coatings have been developed to preserve the sheen. Most of these coatings are lacquers that do not hold up well under the kind of use that faucets receive. Once they scratch or begin to peel, the brass tarnishes rapidly. Recoating is difficult and seldom satisfactory.

More durable coatings, such as polymer resin, are generally worth the extra cost. In some cases, the manufacturer leaves the finish off intentionally so the brass will achieve a soft patina with age. Of course, brass can be kept shiny with regular polishing. Another option is gold plating, which also resists tarnishing.

Colored faucets can add a bright design element. Lacquers are sometimes used for the colored finish, but epoxy resins are more durable.

Faucet styles are as varied as the finishes. When making your selection, consider how well the faucet harmonizes with the rest of the bathroom design. Consider practical matters too. How high is the spout? How easy is it to turn the handles with wet or soapy hands? Do you want the spout to swivel? (If you do, a faucet for a bar or a kitchen sink may work nicely in the bathroom.)

INTERNAL WORKINGS: Faucet mechanisms have advanced a long way beyond the simple valve stem with replaceable washers that wore out every few years (although such faucets are still sold). Precision metal parts, synthetic materials, and hard ceramics have made the washerless faucet commonplace, and on those rare occasions when maintenance is required, the repair is a simple matter of replacing a modular assembly. Ceramic disc faucets can go from off to full torrent in only a quarter turn of the handle.

Any spigot will squirt water. But bathroom faucets can be highly decorative accents for the sink area. Consider form, finish, and function when making your selection.

EXPERT ADVICE

Old brass faucets sometimes contain high levels of lead, a harmful metal when ingested. If you use such a faucet, let the water run a full minute before drinking it. A lead-free faucet is a better choice.

VANITY AREAS

Exposed light bulbs along each side of a mirror offer the right illumination for shaving or applying makeup.

The vanity area offers many opportunities in bathroom design. It's the essence of practicality and should be treated as familiar furniture amid the plumbing fixtures and hard-finished surfaces.

If a vanity is long, taking up one whole wall of the room, it sets a tone of relaxation and repose. If it has a wood finish or rounded edges, it contrasts warmly with porcelain and tile. A traditional dressing table, which has no sink, invites the user to linger rather than rush. The possibilities are almost limitless.

The vanity area includes a lavatory and faucet, countertop, medicine cabinet, and mirrors. Lighting and electrical outlet needs also play a part in determining the final look of your vanity area.

VANITIES

There should be enough room in front of the vanity for the doors and drawers to open and close without interference. There should be enough wall space for a mirror and lighting. If either side of the vanity is exposed and a corner juts out into the room, consider curved edges to prevent painful bumps.

Determine exactly how much storage space you will need and plan spaces for specific items. If you are buying a modular unit, the size of the storage spaces will be predetermined, so make sure it meets your needs. Consider including additional storage, as well. Matching modular units are available from many manufacturers and can create a coordinated ensemble.

TYPES AND SIZES: You can buy a vanity as you would a modular kitchen cabinet, or you can have one custom-designed and built by a cabinet shop. Like kitchen cabinets, vanities come in a wide array of materials, colors, and styles. Some are sold as a package with a countertop of cast polymer or other material with a molded lavatory.

The standard front-to-back depth for a vanity is 18–21 inches. Widths start at 18 inches and continue in 6-inch increments to 72 inches. Matching filler can be used to adapt a standard vanity to fit any space.

Most vanities are 29–30 inches high, including the countertop, but you adjust the height by modifying the base.

ADULTS-ONLY TIP: If the bathroom isn't used by children, consider raising the height of the vanity to 36 inches to make it more comfortable to use.

COUNTERTOPS

Bathroom counters are not confined to the vanity. They can cantilever out from the wall or extend beyond the vanity to create a larger, more useful surface.

MATERIAL CHOICES: Countertops, trim, and backsplash can be made from all sorts of materials. The range of colors, textures, and design possibilities is immense. If you want a countertop with a sink molded into it, choose cast polymer or solid surface material. These basin-countertops provide an integrated, seamless unit. If you want a separate lavatory, choose among plastic laminates, ceramic tile, marble, granite, and wood, as well as solid surface material.

■ CAST POLYMER COUNTERTOPS generally come with the sink molded in. They are available in many colors and are relatively inexpensive. Cast polymer is easy to clean but prone to damage from burns, scratching, and wear.

■ SOLID-SURFACE MATERIAL is more expensive but durable because color and texture are uniform throughout. It comes in a range of colors and designs, in plain slabs or in preformed sink countertops. Stains, scratches, and burns can be removed with sanding. It is sold under such brand names as Avonite, Corian, and Fountainhead.

■ PLASTIC LAMINATES are thin veneers of durable plastic material glued to a stable backing. Available in many colors, patterns, and textures, they are easy to clean and inexpensive. But they scorch and scratch easily and have brittle edges if not fabricated properly. To avoid a dark, distracting seam, choose laminate with solid color throughout, not just in the veneer.

■ CERAMIC TILE is a traditional favorite. Available in a wide range of sizes, shapes, colors, and textures, it's durable, moderately expensive, and lends itself to do-it-yourself installations. It can be individualized with accent pieces or decorative tiles. On the negative side, grout lines can be subject to mildew and staining unless treated properly. Common sizes are 3-inch and 4-inch squares and mosaics 1 to 2 inches in diameter. For a perfect match, order trim pieces at the same time you order regular tiles.

■ MARBLE OR GRANITE SLABS OR SQUARES can be used for countertops. Granite is extremely durable. Marble is easily stained and is susceptible to anything acidic. For this reason, it should be sealed periodically.

■ WOOD must be used with extreme caution in a bathroom, especially for horizontal surfaces, such as countertops. Certain species (such as teak and redwood) are more suitable than others, but all wood must be treated carefully and sealed properly to stand up under normal bathroom use.

DESIGN TIP

Before determining a finish for your vanity area, decide on sink and faucet styles. This will affect some of your tile trim choices.

VANITY AREAS
continued

MEDICINE CABINET

There are options to the familiar box-type medicine cabinet. You might install a large wall mirror and store medicines and toiletries elsewhere. You might place a mirror and a medicine cabinet on adjacent sidewalls to create a mirrored corner.

PRACTICAL CONSIDERATIONS: Most medicine cabinets are designed to be recessed into the wall so that only the thickness of the mirror door protrudes. Surface-mounted cabinets, extending 4–6 inches from the wall, are used where obstacles make it impossible to install a recessed cabinet.

Typical sizes for a single-door cabinet are 15–18 inches wide and 26–36 inches high. Sizes for double- and triple-door units are typically 30, 36, or 48 inches wide and 26 or 34–36 inches high. Larger units may be 54, 60, 72, or 80 inches wide and 36–40 inches high.

You have many options when it comes to mirrors, doors, and shelves. Doors can be hinged or sliding. Most single doors can be reversed to open on the left or the right. Some units are designed for corner installations; others are installed as a pair with a wall mirror between them to create an adjustable three-way mirror. Some units have three mirrors built into the cabinet. Most units have adjustable mirrors and shelves.

Medicine cabinets come frameless and in a wide choice of frames made of chrome, wood, brass, or colored metals. In many, a bar of bulb lights can be installed along the top.

DESIGN TIP

When choosing a medicine cabinet, consider its dimensions and proportions in relation to other features of the room. For example, if you are installing the medicine cabinet above a vanity and mounting a light bar over the top, all three fixtures should align smoothly and be in proportion to one another. If the medicine cabinet is too small, the vanity will overwhelm it. If it is too large, it will draw the eye away from the vanity, diminishing its impact.

SIZING TIP

To plan the size of a mirror, line up top, bottom, and sides with other features of the room—the top of a backsplash, a window sill, a corner where two walls intersect, the top of a door or a window, or a storage unit. This will give a preliminary mirror size to aid planning. To arrive at the exact size, have the installer take on-site measurements before cutting.

MIRRORS

Expanses of mirror must be carefully planned. You can buy mirrors in standard sizes from a building supplier, or a glass shop will cut them to order and install them for you.

The vanity or sink should have a mirror that is well lighted and at a convenient height for everybody who uses it. You may also want a magnifying mirror that can be adjusted to various positions. Another helpful arrangement consists of a stationary center mirror with two hinged side mirrors that swing to adjust the viewing angle.

DESIGN CONSIDERATIONS: Mirrors can be used to expand apparent space in a small bathroom or in one that is long and narrow. If one wall is covered with mirror from counter to ceiling, the room will appear twice as large. It also makes everything appear double, which could be distracting. Mirrors on walls that intersect at a corner create a fascinating effect and also tend to double the apparent size of the room. Mirrors on opposite walls create the familiar barbershop tunnel-to-infinity effect. This can be fun for guests, but it might be tedious on a daily basis.

If you want to use mirrors to expand space without overdoing it, the safest approach is to use one or two fairly large mirrors, perhaps 5 feet wide and 3½ feet tall, rather than floor-to-ceiling or wall-to-wall mirrors. If you use one large mirror, place it on a wall that forms a right angle to the entry.

UTILITIES

The need to plan ahead for utilities cannot be overemphasized. From a practical standpoint, these are the most important choices of the entire project.

Well-placed lighting, convenient electrical outlets, reliable heating, and proper ventilation contribute as much to the success of your project as any fixture, fitting, or finish.

ELECTRICAL LIGHTING

Lighting is a dynamic design element, essential for safety and well-being. Without proper light, the most stylish room appears flat and uninteresting. In today's bathroom, a variety of light sources and independent controls are used to create ideal illumination and ambience.

An effective lighting system provides overall illumination for the entire bathroom and concentrated illumination for specific tasks. Start by identifying the areas where light should be concentrated. Usually there is also enough spillover from these task lights to meet general lighting needs.

VANITY FLAIR: The vanity area requires special lighting. A person standing or sitting in front of the mirror should be bathed in soft, shadowless light. A single light source above the mirror will throw harsh shadows. The ideal arrangement is to have lights on both sides of the mirror and a light above it. Side bulbs could be vertical bar lights (sometimes called theater lights or Hollywood lights), vertical fluorescent tubes, or vertical incandescent tubes. Lights should extend from a point approximately 6–12 inches above the countertop to a point about 6–6½ feet above the floor. The overhead light

This gracious bathroom features upper cabinets as well as double vanities. Set countertops at heights tailored for your comfort; sections can be raised as well as lowered from standard.

UTILITIES
continued

could be a fixture in the same style as the side lights, mounted horizontally on the wall above the mirror, or it could consist of two or three recessed ceiling fixtures shining straight down on the vanity top. Light bouncing off the mirror and other surfaces will help to eliminate shadows.

TUB SAFETY: Another important item to illuminate is the bathtub. One or two recessed ceiling fixtures, each 60–75 watts, over the tub are usually sufficient. However, electrical codes typically specify that any electrical device around a tub or whirlpool must be at least $7\frac{1}{2}$ feet above the flood rim of the tub or at least 5 feet away from the tub horizontally. An exception is made for recessed or surface-mounted ceiling fixtures with a glass or plastic lens and no metal rim. Check local building regulations pertaining to bathroom lighting.

Any steps leading up to the tub should be illuminated, either with a recessed ceiling fixture or with low-voltage strip lights mounted under the overhang of each step.

Don't forget to illuminate enclosed areas. For showers with incandescent fixtures, a total of 60 watts is recommended. In the toilet compartment, provide incandescent fixtures of 60–75 watts or fluorescent fixtures of 30–40 watts.

SPECIAL MOODS AND NEEDS: Besides illuminating certain areas for specific tasks, a good lighting system provides enough ambient light to eliminate shadows and stark contrasts and to illuminate the floor to prevent falls. Use dimmers and switching for mood and spotlighting.

The type of light you use will affect ambience and perception. Incandescent light is soft and flattering to the complexion. Fluorescent light is harsh and cold if the tubes are cool white. Warm-white and full-spectrum tubes are better for bathroom use.

Different types of rooms require different types of lighting. A powder room can be fairly dark and lends itself to dramatic lighting. A bathroom where grooming and other exact tasks are performed must be well lit.

Consider, too, the users' special needs. A bathroom for older adults, who are sensitive to glare and require higher light intensities, must have excellent illumination. The easiest solution is to use a color scheme with light, reflective colors and to increase the wattage capacity of the fixtures.

Be sure that all electrical devices in a bathroom are served by GFCI (Ground Fault Circuit Interrupter) breakers and outlets.

DESIGN TIP

For grooming, lights should be placed on both sides as well as above the mirror. Illumination on each side should total approximately 75–120 watts for incandescent lights and 20 watts for fluorescent tubes. Overhead lights should total 100–120 incandescent watts, or 32–54 fluorescent watts.

NATURALLY RADIANT

Look for ways to bring as much natural daylight into the room as possible. Think about adding or enlarging windows to incorporate views and available light. Bear in mind that light from only one source creates glare and high contrasts, so try to plan another window on a different wall or use a skylight to provide balance.

Skylights admit five times as much light as a window of the same size. Because most bathrooms are small, even a skylight 2 feet square will have a dramatic impact.

Converting a window to a French door or a miniature greenhouse is another excellent way to gain sunlight as well as style. A corner window provides a double light source in addition to an attractive setting for a bathtub.

If the need for privacy makes ordinary windows unacceptable, use diffuse glass or glass block, or place the windows high enough in the wall to preserve privacy.

Some windows receive intense sunlight during certain times of the day and during certain seasons. For example, morning sun and winter sun are usually welcome, but you may need to provide shades to soften the light. A west-facing window exposed to afternoon sun and a clear skylight should be shaded during the summer months.

If the window is in a bathtub or shower

LIGHT TIP

Lighting is a complex science. Consider hiring a lighting consultant to help determine your needs. Obtain referrals from your local lighting store and from friends who have remodeled.

enclosure, use clear glass doors or a clear plastic shower curtain to let as much light into the room as possible. When planning windows around tubs and showers, keep safety in mind. Local codes specify how close you can carry standard window glass to the floor or to the rim of the tub. Beyond that point, you must use tempered glass, safety plate, or other approved glazing.

HEATING

Bathrooms usually require more heat than other rooms in the house. Where a comfortable temperature for most rooms is around 70° F, a bathroom is comfortable at 86° F. It is difficult and costly to maintain temperatures this high, so other heating strategies must be considered.

In planning a heating system, it is helpful to understand how the body perceives heat. Heat is constantly moving from warm objects to cooler objects. It can be transferred by conduction, convection, or radiation.

■ CONDUCTION is the direct transfer of heat through a solid medium (for example, by touching a hot stove).

■ CONVECTION is transfer of heat through the air (for example, by means of a forced-air heating system).

■ RADIATION is the direct transfer of heat across space. If you stand in direct sunshine, you feel heat from the sun; as soon as you move into shade, you no longer feel heat. Conversely, the body radiates heat directly toward the cooler objects surrounding it. This is especially true of unclothed portions of the body. It is this transfer of heat through radiation that affects your comfort the most. If the air temperature is 60° F but you are surrounded by surfaces averaging 90° F, you body will not radiate heat toward those surfaces very rapidly, and you will feel warm.

A radiant heating system is ideal for a bathroom because it warms the surfaces in the room first and the air only indirectly. An electric heat mat can be layed under a ceramic tile floor to keep bare toes toasty. An electric wall heater, a baseboard heater, or radiant-heat lamps can be run at high intensity for a short time to create a radiant-heat source that directly warms the body. The alternative, heating the air, would take much longer.

If it is not possible to install a radiant-heating system in the bathroom, the options

are to increase the output of the forced-air system by enlarging the duct or adding a new register, or to expand the hot-water system by adding a new radiator.

If your budget is limited and your bathroom heating needs amount to only an occasional cold morning or evening, consider a portable heater. Be sure you have a safe electrical outlet and storage for the heater.

You may want to consult with a specialist to determine the best type of heating system for your bathroom. If your current system works well, keep it intact or move a register or two, if necessary.

STAY OUT OF HOT WATER

Creating another bathroom only creates another problem if you run out of hot water. If your water heater is in another part of the house, it may take a long time to reach the new bathroom. Your water heater may or may not be up to the challenge of supplying yet another bathroom.

Among ways to solve this problem:
■ Insulate the hot-water pipes
■ Run a continuous loop of hot-water piping (through which the hot water constantly circulates)
■ Install a second water heater closer to the bathroom

Electric tank heaters can be installed almost anywhere because they require no flue, and the 240-volt electrical line is much easier to run than the pipeline for a gas model. Gas and electric tankless water heaters heat water as it runs through the unit. They heat any amount of water and are small enough to fit inside a vanity or a small cabinet.

BUYER'S GUIDE

Consider purchasing towel warmers that are plumbed directly to the hot-water lines. These store instant hot water for the shower or tub in addition to heating your towels while you bathe.

UTILITIES
continued

ELECTRICAL OUTLETS

For your bathroom to work efficiently, electrical outlets must be easily accessible:
■ Provide at least one duplex receptacle outlet near the mirror to accommodate hair dryers, razors, and other grooming appliances.
■ Consider putting an outlet inside one of the cabinets.
■ Provide an outlet at floor level for vacuum cleaners, waxers, and other needs.
■ If plans call for an exhaust fan, clock, radio, TV, towel warmer, or a 240-volt heater, be sure to include suitable electrical service.
■ A special air switch or similar device is recommended for a whirlpool. Spa, sauna, and whirlpool manufacturers' brochures list the electrical requirements for their equipment.

SOUND CONTROL

Several design and construction techniques can be used to prevent bathroom noises from wafting into other parts of the house. The most effective method is to soundproof the walls. This can be done in a variety of ways.

1. If you gut the bathroom and expose the wall framing, the best soundproofing technique is to build a false wall inside the original wall. Stagger the studs so you can weave blanket insulation between them.
2. A simpler but less effective technique is to attach sound insulation board or metal insulating channels to the studs before you apply the wallboard.
3. The least effective technique is to install insulation in the stud cavities. Sound will still carry through the studs.

A careful layout also helps to control sound. Locate closets or built-in cabinet units where they will buffer noises from the bath, and do not place the bathroom door directly opposite the door to another room.

Sound can be controlled with careful construction, as well:
■ Look for spaces where noise may travel through walls, such as cracks along the floor or around electrical outlet boxes, and seal these spaces with caulk, insulation, or foam.
■ Strap water pipes securely and wrap drainpipes in insulation to dampen noise.
■ Insulate around the bathtub, both to control noise and to help retain heat.

SAFETY TIP

By code, all bathroom outlets, switches, and light fixtures must be protected with ground-fault circuit interrupters (GFCIs). These inexpensive devices prevent electrical shock if installed properly and tested regularly.

■ If sound travels through heating ducts, line the first few feet of duct with special fiberglass insulating board to absorb sound.

VENTILATION

A bathroom must have adequate ventilation to prevent the buildup of moisture, mildew, and odors. An operable window fulfills most code requirements for bathroom ventilation, but an exhaust fan ducted directly to the outside—not just to the attic—is a practical necessity. It can be installed in the ceiling or in the exterior wall and should have its own

THREE WAYS TO BLOCK NOISE

1 *Build a false wall inside the original wall, staggering the studs so you can weave blanket insulation between them.*

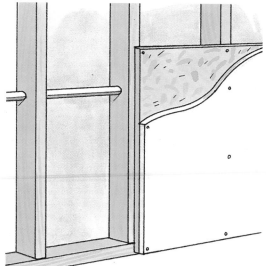

2 *Attach sound insulation board or metal insulating channels to the studs before you apply the wallboard.*

In cold climates where an open window is undesirable, the only way to bring fresh air into the bathroom may be with an air-to-air heat exchanger. This device draws stale air out of the house, draws in fresh air, and uses the heat from the former to warm the latter. In a cold climate, fit the exhaust fan with a damper to prevent the back flow of cold air when the fan is not in use.

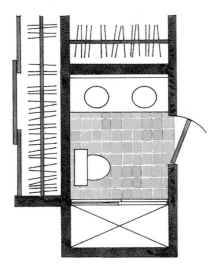

3 *Locate closets or built-in cabinet units where they will buffer noises from the bathroom.*

BUYER'S GUIDE

To determine the minimum cfm rating for an exhaust fan:
- Calculate your bathroom's volume in cubic feet (length × width × height)
- Multiply this by 8 (the desired number of air exchanges per hour)
- Divide the resulting number by 60 (the number of minutes in an hour).

A skylight funnels natural light into this airy bath. Textured glass block allows a measure of privacy without shutting out the light or locking in the humidity.

separate switch. Some fans are incorporated into a light fixture and have separate switches for the fan and the light.

Make sure the fan you buy is not the recirculating type, which merely recycles air so all the moisture remains inside the house.

If the ceiling is pitched, try to locate the fan at the highest point. If there is a skylight well, you might locate a fan there. Otherwise, place it as near the shower or tub as possible.

Fans are rated by volume of air they move in one minute, measured as cubic feet per minute (CFM). The minimum size for most bathrooms is 50 CFM, but larger units are available. Consult the manufacturer's recommendations to determine the appropriate size for your room.

Fans are also rated for sound, measured in units called *sones*. A sound level of 4 sones or less is desirable. Roof-mounted fans tend to be quieter than ceiling-mounted fans.

Although a window provides ventilation and lets in fresh air, it may not exhaust steam and vapor efficiently if it faces into the prevailing breezes. The best method for removing moisture without a fan is to install a working skylight. Motorized units open and close automatically. Manual units are cranked open by means of a long handle.

CONSTRUCTION TIP

Look in home centers for insulation and wallboard fasteners specifically designed to deaden sound.

FINISH MATERIALS

The floor, walls, ceiling, and window treatments are major visual features of a bathroom, but they do not necessarily require dramatic or exotic finishes.

Finish materials must not only look good, they must function well. Therefore, practical considerations—such as moisture resistance and ease of maintenance—should influence your choices.

FLOOR COVERINGS

A bathroom floor should be safe, comfortable, water-resistant, beautiful, and easy to maintain. No single floor covering is ideal for all bathrooms. Each one has certain advantages and disadvantages, which you must weigh when you make your final choice.

DESIGN CONSIDERATIONS: The floor anchors the design, tying all the elements together and highlighting the room's dominant features. In some cases, a bold or unusual floor can be a dominant feature in itself, but in most bathrooms the floor plays a background role.

Because most bathrooms are small, bathroom floors lend themselves to strategies for making a small space appear larger. The most important consideration is color. Light, neutral colors make a space feel larger. Using the same color for both floor and walls helps to expand the space even more. If the flooring has a pattern, it should be simple and uniformly textured. A bold pattern tends to overwhelm a small space. If you use tile, choose grout of the same or similar color to make the floor appear larger; a contrasting color emphasizes the grid pattern and may make the floor—and the room—look small.

Dark colors can appear warm and rich, even cozy and intimate. However, they tend to show water spots, spills, and stains more readily than light colors.

PRACTICAL CONSIDERATIONS: Some materials may raise the level of the finished floor above that of the floor in adjacent rooms. Most flooring materials are quite thin, and the difference in floor heights can usually be bridged with a threshold or a transition piece in the doorway. Be sure to consider the thickness of the underlayment when you determine the height of the new floor. Floor tiles set in a mortar bed can be as much as 1½ inches thick. Brick or masonry units are also thick. If you want a smooth floor between rooms, you may have to drop the level of the subfloor when you use these materials.

Make sure the floor structure is strong enough to support such heavy materials as masonry or stone or a tile floor set in a mortar bed. Even if the floor unit itself is structurally sound, any deflection or movement could cause cracking in the finished floor.

MATERIALS: Your choice of flooring will depend on your specific needs as well as your personal preferences.

■ CERAMIC TILE is water-resistant, durable, easy to clean, and comes in a wide choice of colors and styles, including non-skid surfaces. It conducts heat rapidly and reflects sounds easily. However, because it's hard, objects dropped on it will break.

Sizes range from ½-inch mosaics to 12-inch squares, but 4-inch, 8-inch, and 12-inch squares are common. For moisture-resistance, unglazed tiles must be sealed after installation. If you use different sized tiles for the walls, lay the floor tiles diagonally so mismatched grout lines will not be distracting.

■ DIMENSIONED-STONE TILES are cut from granite, slate, marble, or other natural stone. They resemble ceramic tile but possess the random patterns and subtle variations of a natural material. Slate tends to be dark gray or green. Marble ranges from pure white and stark black to rich shades of salmon, rose, and green. Granite is typically a mottled black and white, but can have a rose or green tint. Because polished finishes can be very slippery when wet, dull or matte finishes are more suitable for bathroom floors. Marble stains easily and must be sealed. Typically, stone tiles come in 12-inch squares.

Ceramic and stone tiles in a wet area should be laid over special tile-backing units, if using a thinset installation. This makes installation easier and extends the tiles' life.

■ RESILIENT SHEET MATERIALS, such as vinyl and linoleum, are inexpensive, skid-resistant, water-resistant, and easy to maintain. They have a cushioned backing, come in a wide array of patterns and colors, and can be installed in most bathrooms with few seams. They are sold by the roll in 6-foot, 12-foot, and occasionally 9-foot widths. The best materials also have a wear layer—a clear layer of vinyl or urethane laid down over the pattern. For a high-traffic bathroom, choose a pattern that will not scratch easily.

■ RESILIENT TILES are made of vinyl, rubber, or cork. They are usually the least expensive flooring and the easiest to install, but they resist moisture poorly due to many seams.

■ CARPET is the softest floor covering, but doesn't take moisture well. Bathroom carpet

should have a synthetic backing with a pad of synthetic foam material (such as a rebond padding) to keep moisture from soaking through. In wet areas, such as in front of the tub, use water-resistant material, such as tile.
■ WOOD FLOORS can be used if they are sealed with several coats of polyurethane or a similar durable finish. However, even properly sealed wood floors are vulnerable to moisture over time. They are best used in powder rooms or in the drier parts of a bathroom. Square-edged seams withstand moisture better than tongue-and-groove seams.

MAINTENANCE TIP

All floor coverings must be cleaned regularly and some require periodic maintenance.
■ Carpet should be washed frequently to control must and mildew.
■ Marble must be sealed periodically to protect it from stains.
■ Tile grout must be sealed to control both stains and mildew.
■ Resilient flooring, while easy to maintain, may wear out sooner than other materials.
■ Wood floors are sealed with hard finishes that should be renewed every few years.

Create unique and playful accents with ceramic tile as flooring material, as shown below.

Ceramic tile provides a low-maintenance, waterproof wainscoting and floor in the bath shown in the inset photo.

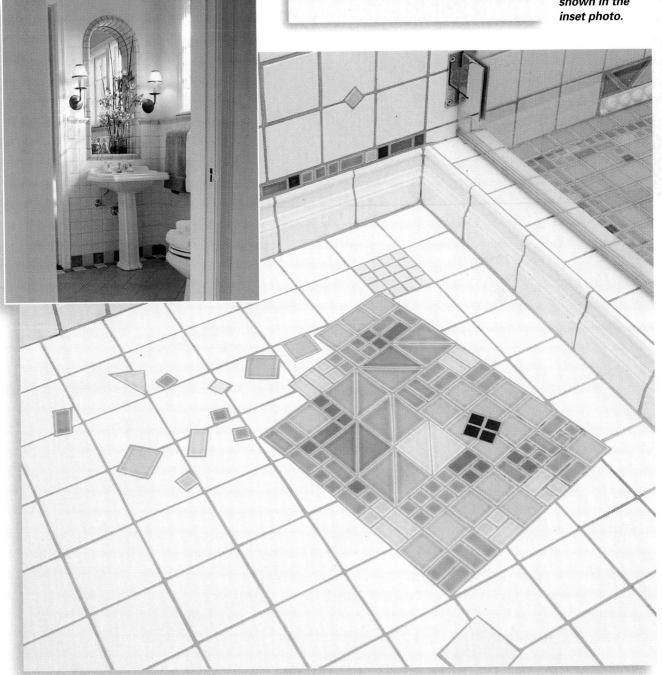

FINISH MATERIALS
continued

WALLS

The largest surface area of a bathroom is the walls, although windows, doorways, storage units, shower stalls, vanities, and fixtures reduce this area considerably. Finish materials should be chosen for their appearance, moisture resistance, and ease of maintenance. Mixing materials for their strengths in different areas works well, especially in a compartmented bathroom.

The area around the tub or shower is especially important. Because it is subject to direct water contact, it should be finished with materials that are completely waterproof. The backing on finish materials is equally important; for most shower and tub installations it consists either of a mortar bed or tile-backed units. Special moisture-resistant wallboard is sometimes used, but it has largely been replaced by tile-backed units. The rest of the walls can be covered with standard wallboard.

PAINT: The least expensive wall treatment for bathrooms is paint. It comes in an unlimited range of colors and is easy to apply. Choose a high quality paint in either a gloss or semi-gloss finish, which repels water and

Specialty painting techniques can transform an ordinary bath into a work of art.

cleans easily. Most surfaces must be primed to assure proper adhesion. Paint alone is not suitable for shower or tub enclosures exposed to direct spray.

WALLCOVERINGS: Vinyl and similar plastic wallcoverings can be effective in bathrooms. Ordinary wallpaper and foil papers can be used if they are not subjected to direct water or heavy condensation. None of these papers is suitable for shower or tub surrounds.

TILE: The classic wall finish for bathrooms is ceramic tile, especially for tub and shower enclosures and around other plumbing fixtures. Tile has a smooth, durable surface that resists moisture, is easy to clean, and looks new for many years. Wall tiles (which are usually thinner and more brittle than floor tiles) come in a vast array of colors and patterns that can be combined to produce a variety of effects.

Stone tiles can be used on vertical surfaces, providing they are not too thick. Check with the dealer or the installer during the planning stage to make certain the tiles you choose are thin enough to stay on the walls.

SLAB MATERIALS: Large slabs of natural marble, granite, cultured marble, or solid surface materials can create luxurious-looking walls with few seams. These walls resist moisture and are easy to clean, although marble will stain if it is not sealed properly. Many slab materials are expensive and should be installed professionally. Though used most commonly in showers and tub surrounds, they can also look dramatic on other wall surfaces. Slabs of natural stone are extremely heavy, so if you plan to use stone extensively, have an architect, structural engineer, or contractor check the structure of the walls and floor to determine whether they should be reinforced.

LAMINATES: High-pressure plastic laminates, often used in cabinets and countertops, can also cover walls. The intense colors and durable surface allow creation of exciting effects. Laminates come in 4-foot widths, often wide enough to make a seamless installation.

CEILINGS

Don't overlook the ceiling. It's an important design element.

Any variation from a standard 8-foot flat ceiling adds interest and drama to a room. However, variations must be used carefully in a bathroom. A high ceiling makes most rooms feel formal, where a bathroom should feel intimate and relaxed. A high ceiling may also overwhelm a small bathroom. If the ceiling is too high, you can create the illusion of a lower ceiling by adding a painted or tiled border strip around the wall at the 8-foot level. You can even install a false ceiling.

A skylight or other interruption acts as a focal point. Beams and soffits can alter the apparent shape of a room. A beam running across the narrow dimension of a long room makes it feel more square, for example, or a soffit can define a tub or vanity area, creating a place to conceal recessed light fixtures.

A bathroom ceiling can be finished with any material used on walls, except heavy slabs and most wallpapers. Because a full tile ceiling can feel institutional, tile on ceilings is usually restricted to tub or shower enclosures. Ceilings of cedar, redwood, or similar durable wood can work well in a bathroom, giving it a natural or rustic appearance. Semi-gloss paint and wallcoverings are the most popular bathroom finishes and the least expensive.

FINISH MATERIALS
continued

WINDOW TREATMENTS

To be effective, the window and window treatment must harmonize with the overall design. Size and location of a window; the type, style, and shape of the frame and glass; and window coverings need to be planned.

Start by choosing the type of glass. If the view is pleasant and privacy is not an issue, use clear glass. Otherwise, choose diffused glass, which has a frosted, translucent quality. One-way, or mirrored, glass is another option. It presents a reflective surface to the outside but lets you see out. If the window is exposed to intense sunlight during hot weather, consider tinted, heat-reflecting glass.

Dress up an ordinary window with stained glass. The simplest way to do this is to hang a stained glass panel in front of the window. For a permanent installation, remove the window sash and replace the original pane with a custom-made stained glass design.

Other window treatments include shutters, blinds, and curtains. Wood shutters should be painted with a gloss or semi-gloss paint or, if stained, sealed with polyurethane to protect them against moisture damage. Choose solid brass hardware or some other finish that won't rust in a humid bathroom. If the hardware is steel (you can find out by checking it with a magnet), coat it with a clear plastic sealer to prevent discoloration.

Blinds add a touch of contemporary elegance to a bathroom. Some double-glazed windows come with microblinds installed between the panes. When you buy window blinds for a bathroom, choose high-quality products with a plastic coating, otherwise the metal slats may rust.

Curtains add a note of romance and soften hard surfaces. Most fabrics can withstand bathroom humidity as long as the room is heated and ventilated properly. A good fabric dealer can help you make the best selection for your specific bathroom.

MAINTENANCE TIP

Bathrooms are, by nature, humid places (unless it's a powder room without a tub or shower). Make sure the window covering you choose can withstand moisture and humid conditions.

If you can't fit enough windows into conventional side walls, think about adding a skylight, clerestory, or half-round window near the ceiling.

PLANNING ACCESSORIES

Many beautiful, luxurious bathrooms were completed before anyone realized that there was no place to hang a towel. On a day-to-day basis, simple accessories are among important features of a bathroom. Among the most common:

- A hamper or laundry chute
- Storage units
- Toilet paper holder
- Soap dish
- Magazine and book racks
- Bathtub toy storage for a family bathroom
- Holders for toothbrushes and a tumbler
- Caddies for shower accessories
- Bathrobe hooks

Include these in your plans. If you assume they can be added later, your sleek design may be overwhelmed by a clutter of small details.

TOWEL BARS

First look for available wall space on which to mount towel bars. Standard lengths are 18, 24, 30, 36, and 42 inches. A comfortable height is 36–48 inches, although higher bars are acceptable above a countertop. Where wall space is limited, towel rings are an option, especially for hand towels.

Be sure to include enough space for the towels to hang: at least 18 inches below the bar for a hand towel, 12 inches for a guest towel, and 30 inches for a bath towel.

If there is not enough wall space to hang towels, or if you do not want to display them prominently, consider mounting towel bars on the back of a door, the side of a vanity, or inside a well-ventilated closet.

GRAB BARS

Grab bars are a sensible addition to any bathroom, in the shower, tub, and beside the toilet. Make sure they're anchored to framing studs, not just screwed or glued to wallboard.

STORAGE

First identify your needs. Decide exactly what you want in the bathroom, where it should go, and how much space it will require.

CLOSETS: High on most people's wish list is a large closet, with shelves for towels and space to hang robes and clothing. If there is a bedroom closet on the backside of one bathroom wall, you may be able to partition part of it and put a door in the wall. If there is space at the end of the bathtub or in a corner, you may be able to build a new closet.

Wardrobe closets are usually 24 inches deep, but a shallower closet will hold shelves and a couple of clothes hooks. Another option is to buy a prefabricated modular unit.

CABINETS: Several types of modular cabinets are designed for bathrooms: wall units, hampers, base units that double as seats, and tall storage units. Many standard kitchen cabinets can also be used in the bathroom. Base units are 24 inches deep, and wall units are 12 inches deep; widths range from 18 to 48 inches in 3-inch increments. If space is tight, cut down a wall unit. Even a cabinet 8 inches deep will hold towels and supplies.

Custom cabinets can be built to fit any space. They usually look less obtrusive than single modular units because they can be aligned with other features in the room and finished with the same materials.

Antique dressers, armoires, china cabinets, or collection cases are appropriate in many bathroom settings, and need not fit perfectly to look extremely handsome. However, consider the effects of moisture.

SHELVES: Some accessories are best stored on open shelves. A set of shelves can be hung above the toilet or below a window. Single shelves can go almost anywhere and be any size, from a narrow glass unit above the sink to a continuous shelf across one whole wall.

Shelves can also be built into walls. A simple alcove finished in plaster makes a stunning display for rolled-up towels.

RUGS

No matter which floor covering you choose, plan for some kind of rug to step on after a shower or bath. Be sure the rug you choose is backed with a skid-proof surface.

ART

Sculpture, ceramics, art glass, and other durable pieces can generally withstand the most extreme conditions and are ideal for bathrooms. A properly ventilated bathroom, where the temperature is stable and moisture is controlled, may be appropriate for framed prints, some oil paintings, photographs, and fabric works. Consult with a professional artist, collector, or restorer before displaying valuable paintings and drawings in bathrooms.

OTHER OPTIONS

Other accessories to consider include a radio, telephone, television, stereo, furniture, and a fitness center.

PLANNING FOR SAFETY

Help prevent accidents with safety-conscious design and by taking safety precautions. Start with a floor plan that allows freedom of movement. Choose skid-resistant floor covering. Finally, use common sense.

CHECKLIST

■ Do not have a raised tub requiring steps. If steps are necessary, equip them with handrails and a slip-resistant surface.
■ Avoid sharp edges in the bathroom.
■ To prevent burns, set the thermostat on your water heater no higher than 120 degrees.
■ Provide lockable storage for medications.
■ Store cleaning agents and other dangerous materials out of youngsters' reach.
■ Protect all electrical outlets with GFCI devices.
■ Provide enough outlets to eliminate the use of extension cords.
■ Place light switches at heights convenient to every member of the family.
■ Do not store items used daily in hard-to-reach places.
■ Avoid one-step changes in floor level.
■ Be sure all floor and task areas are well lighted.
■ Get proper permits for all work done on the bathroom.
■ Install electrical fixtures, appliances, and whirlpool equipment according to manufacturers' instructions and local code.
■ Install a door lock that can be easily opened from the outside.
■ Plan doors that do not swing open into a corridor and (if possible) will not be blocked by someone who has fallen on the floor.
■ Use temperature control faucets in the shower, tub, and lavatory.
■ Provide a security lock on any window that may be left partially open.
■ Maintain privacy by blocking any view from a public area with fencing or some other screening device.

ALLOW ENOUGH ROOM

In planning a bathroom layout, know what minimum clearances are required between the plumbing fixtures. In a design where fractions of an inch count, it may be tempting to squeeze the fixtures too close together so that everything fits. You must maintain the minimum clearances for safety and comfort.

Your local building department can give you the code requirements for your area, but the following guidelines are typical of most codes. Try to allow more space than the code requires. These are minimum standards. They do not guarantee that the room won't feel cramped.

TOILET

Allow at least 15 inches from the centerline of the toilet to a wall or bathtub on the side. A toilet compartment must therefore be at least 30 inches wide between finish walls, but 36 inches is better. If there is a sink beside the toilet, there should be at least 4 inches of clearance between the two fixtures. Allow at least 21 inches of free space in front of the toilet; 24 inches is more realistic.

Provide as much space for a bidet as for a toilet. Because bidets are usually installed adjacent to toilets, be especially careful of the space between the two fixtures. Allow at least 15 inches of clearance between the two bowls.

SINK

There should be at least 21 inches of clearance—preferably 24 inches—in front of a sink. If the sink is beside a bathtub, allow at least 6 inches between the two fixtures.

SHOWER STALL

Shapes and dimensions vary, but the floor of the shower pan should be large enough to contain a disc 34 inches in diameter. In addition, there should be at least 24 inches of clearance in front of the opening for stepping in and out.

BATHTUB

Allow space to get in and out easily. Also consider space for an adult to stand when helping a bathing child. Think about bath mat sizes and allow enough space in front of the tub for a good-sized rug. If you are planning to use a prefabricated shower or bathtub surround, be sure to get the dimensions and clearances from the manufacturer. Side clearances for tubs vary, but keep in mind space for doors, curtains and rods, or a wing wall to block shower spray.

FINALIZING THE DESIGN

It may take months to refine the bathroom plan, but there will come a time when you are ready to produce the final drawings and material specifications.

Finalizing your design includes drawing a detailed floor plan and elevations, and preparing a list of all materials and fixtures you need. You may need only a floor plan to obtain a permit for a simple remodeling project, but you will need the elevations and the specifications list if you consult with a designer, work up a detailed estimate, solicit bids, coordinate subcontractors, and receive material deliveries.

FINAL PLAN

Once you are happy with a particular preliminary plan, you need to make sure the dimensions will actually work within the room. Take a clean copy of your base plan and indicate the exact locations of all fixtures, cabinets, electrical outlets, and other built-in items. Measure carefully. Use the manufacturer's brochures for the exact dimensions of any fixtures or cabinets you have ordered but have yet to receive. When they are delivered, be sure to verify that they are exactly the size you expected.

Be sure to indicate any new water and sewer lines and changes in electrical and telephone lines. Include door swings and wall thicknesses in your drawings.

You may need to make several copies of the final plan for your local building department, inspectors, and workers. If you are remodeling and have a file of the architectural plans of your house, attach these drawings to the file, especially if utility lines will be affected.

ELEVATION DRAWINGS

After completing the final floor plan, make elevation drawings of the walls. Use a separate sheet of paper for each wall and label them north, south, east, and west. Start with floor plan dimensions and complete the elevations by taking field measurements as you go. Include doors, fixtures, shelves, and other major features of the room. Do not include anything you plan to get rid of. If you're not sure, draw it in. You needn't bother drawing in hardware and other fine details, except to experiment with options.

MATERIAL SPECIFICATIONS

Using your cost estimate lists and final floor plan as a starting point, make up a final materials list including all the information you need to order specific items. Noting something as "white countertop" is no longer sufficient. You must know exactly the material, brand, and color of each item.

This list will also serve as a tracking system. Using this list, you'll be able to plan deliveries and storage needs, tell workers when they can expect materials, and adjust other elements if a desired item become unavailable. Update this list regularly and keep it handy.

Some people will find this list more valuable in chart form, especially if it is to be used by several people, such as you, your designer, your contractor, and various subcontractors.

Be sure to indicate the date of all orders and changes. For each item, you'll find it helpful to have the following information:

- Item
- Manufacturer
- Name and model number
- Color, including any name and dye lot
- Material
- Size or measurements
- Quantity
- Unit price
- Total price, including tax and delivery
- Date ordered
- Place ordered
- Name of person through whom you ordered
- Projected date of delivery
- Actual date of delivery
- Second choice
- Items affected by change
- Attach any order receipts

CONSIDER THE DISABLED

A bathroom for disabled access should include a lower tub, an adjustable showerhead, and grab bars.
- For wheelchair use, the door should be at least 32 inches wide. Provide at least 44 inches of hallway clearance for turning into the doorway. Within the bathroom there must be at least 60 inches of clearance in which to turn around.
- The toilet should have 32 inches of clear space on one side and 48 inches in front, with grab bars on both sides.
- Shower stalls should be 60 inches in diameter and have a bench or seat and no curb. Smaller stalls can be fitted with grab bars. Include a shower seat, nonslip grab bars, a single-handle lever control, and a hand-held sprayer.
- The lavatory should have clearance under the basin so a wheelchair can pull up close.
- Faucet handles should be easy to reach. Some have levers long enough to be operated by the wrists or forearms.

This simple country bath is perfect in every way—from its robin's-egg blue walls to its pie safe for towel storage; from an old-fashioned tub to a braided rag rug.

PROJECT PLANNING

Planning for construction is a critical stage in any remodeling. You may be tempted to begin construction as soon as the design stage is completed, but don't do it! A successful project depends on planning everything in advance. Whether you manage the project yourself or hire a general contractor, construction should not begin until you have:

■ A firm estimate of costs

■ Adequate financing

■ A realistic time line

■ A clear understanding of who will be doing what

■ The materials required to complete the job

■ Proper permits

To some extent, any remodeling is a journey into the unknown. Planning every aspect as thoroughly as possible is the best way to avoid surprises, setbacks, and disappointments. The more effort you put into these preliminary tasks, the more successful and enjoyable the project will be.

ESTIMATING EXPENSES

One of the most difficult skills in construction is estimating the cost of the project. An accurate estimate requires final plans and material specifications. You can estimate costs using the principles outlined in this section, or you can hire a contractor to work up an estimate.

Do not rely on your own preliminary plans, a designer's estimate of costs, or any contractor's price that is not a firm bid based on the final plans. Plans and specifications should include:
■ All proposed changes to the structure
■ Locations of all plumbing, electrical, heating, and ventilating devices
■ Type of flooring, wall, and ceiling materials
■ Trim details
■ Window and door specifications
■ Cabinet sizes
■ Model and manufacturer of each plumbing and electrical fixture.

These specifications will enable you and the contractor, subcontractors, suppliers, and consultants to account for every detail.

CONTRACTORS' BIDS

If you are hiring a general contractor or subcontractors, their bids will be the estimate. Be sure you understand what is and is not included in each bid. For instance, who will be responsible for removing debris? For purchasing and installing fixtures? For painting? If your plans do not specify such details as type of tile, brand of faucet, or type of cabinet hardware, clarify whether the bids include a certain allowance for these items. If the bids assume use of cheap materials, expect to pay the difference for more expensive items. Also, try to identify places where problems may arise or where you may opt for additions requiring a change order. This also involves extra expense.

DOING YOUR OWN ESTIMATE

If you are acting as your own general contractor, you will need to do estimate the cost yourself. There are several methods for estimating costs, including the popular method of using square footage multiples and comparing your project to similar projects of known costs. However, the only reliable way to estimate a job is to break it down into

COSTS

If the project involves remodeling an existing bathroom, allow for the unexpected. Quite often, what starts out as a simple rejuvenation project becomes more involved once demolition begins. Surprises may include more involved plumbing changes than you anticipated, unexpected damage from water or insects, or a desire to make additional changes after the project begins.

separate phases, itemize the materials and labor costs for each phase, total them up, and add a reasonable contingency factor.

If you plan to hire subcontractors for some of the work, use their bids as estimates for those phases. For the rest of the project, use a work sheet similar to the one on page 47, basing it on your plans and on construction information in the next chapter. To price materials, make a complete list and make comparisons at various suppliers.

The cost estimate should include a contingency factor, usually 5 to 10 percent, to cover cost overruns.

OBTAINING FINANCING

Unless you're able to pay for a new bathroom out of pocket, you will need to do some financial planning to determine your budget and arrange financing. To help set a realistic budget (and to show to potential lenders), gather the following information:
■ Your net worth (a balance sheet listing the value of assets and the amounts of debts—the difference between total assets and total debt is your net worth.
■ Anticipated new expenses (a baby, a car, college tuition)
■ Your expected cash flow during the design and construction phases (and afterwards, if you are seeking a long-term loan).

Don't forget to consider the value of your home, both now and after you have remodeled the bathroom. If you need help, consult with a local real estate agent or hire a professional appraiser.

Once you have determined your budget and estimated the cost of the project, obtain the financing early enough so that funds will be available when you begin construction.

SAMPLE BREAKDOWN FOR INSTALLING BATHTUB AND SHOWER

Task	Materials	Tools	Labor
Alter framing	2×4s, 1×4s, nails	Hammer, saw, tape measure	½ hour
Rough in drain	1½" P-trap, pipe, fittings, glue	Pipe cutter, tape measure	½ hour
Rough in supply pipes and valve	Faucet, ½" pipe and fittings, faucet, stubs	Pipe cutter or saw, pipe-joining materials, wrenches, tape measure	1 hour
Install tub	Bathtub, shims	Dolly, runners	½ hour
Hook up drain	Trip-lever unit, putty, Teflon tape	Wrenches, screwdrivers, hacksaw	1 hour
Insulate tub	Blanket insulation	Knife	¼ hour
Insulate wall	Insulation, plastic sheeting, staples	Knife, tape measure, stapler	½ hour
Prepare for tile	Tile backing board, nails, tape, corner bead, joint compound, sealer	Knife, hammer, tape measure, joint knife	1 hour
Paint (touch up)	Primer, finish coat, thinner	Brushes, roller, drop cloth	½ hour
Install tile	Adhesive, tile, trim pieces, spacers	Buckets, tile cutter, tape measure, nippers, trowel	3 hours
Grout tile	Grout, additive	Buckets, rubber float, sponges, cheesecloth	2 hours
Install finish plumbing	Faucet flange and handles, spout, showerhead	Screwdrivers, wrenches	¼ hour
Apply caulk	Silicone caulk	Caulking gun, rags	½ hour

HIDDEN COSTS TO WATCH CLOSELY

Most of the costs of a building project are predictable; costs for remodeling are less so. Although most items are in the design plans, there are hidden costs. These are easy to overlook and can add up significantly over the course of a long project.

Hidden costs include:

- Permit fees
- Employer expenses for hiring labor (payroll taxes, Workers' Compensation insurance)
- Tools, either to buy or to rent
- Sharpening or replacing blades
- Power cords and lights
- Safety equipment: goggles, gloves, dust masks, painter's masks, respirators, work boots, hard hats
- Vehicle mileage, wear and tear
- Increased use of telephone and utilities
- Debris box rental or dump fees
- Tarps or plastic sheeting to cover supplies or to protect surfaces
- Replacing inadequate plumbing lines "while we're at it"
- Replacing baseboards to go with new flooring
- Inability to recycle existing materials as originally planned
- Patching the roof or siding around new plumbing vents, duct outlets, windows, or skylights
- Enlarging a deck or porch to accommodate new exterior doors
- Delivery charges for materials
- Insulating exterior walls you hadn't intended to open up
- Cleanup
- New window coverings, accessories, plants

SCHEDULING THE PROJECT

A detailed time line helps you negotiate contracts, schedule your time, and estimate the date of completion. The actual sequence will vary from job to job, but this stage-by-stage depiction is typical of most bathroom projects not involving major structural changes.

PRECONSTRUCTION

1. Complete design
2. Obtain bids or work up an estimate
3. Prepare a time line
4. Arrange for financing
5. Hire a contractor or subcontractors
6. Order materials and fixtures with long delivery times
7. Obtain permits
8. Make arrangements to use another bathroom, if necessary
9. Arrange for debris removal, material storage, and daily cleaning of the path between the work area and the outside.

DEMOLITION

10. Clear out all movable items
11. Seal off the bathroom from other rooms
12. Remove shelves and built-in storage
13. Remove sink, countertop, vanity
14. Remove trim and moldings
15. Remove toilet and seal drain opening
16. Remove or repair floor covering
17. Remove lights and electrical fixtures
18. Remove wall and ceiling finish materials
19. Remove bathtub or shower pan

PREPARING THE SPACE

20. Alter walls; shore up bearing walls
21. Repair subfloor
22. Complete rough framing for alterations, new walls, soffits, windows, doors
23. Install windows, skylights, and doors
24. Install heating and venting ducts
25. Alter or install rough plumbing
26. Install new tub, shower, or shower pan
27. Alter or install rough wiring
28. Install fan
29. Get preliminary inspections
30. Install insulation and get it inspected
31. Repair, replace, or install wallboard and apply finish
32. Install door and window trim, except where it will be fitted around cabinets

33. Paint ceiling, walls, trim
34. Install finish wall coverings
35. Install flooring, including underlayment (some types of flooring may be installed later)
36. Install interior doors

INSTALLING FINISH MATERIALS/FIXTURES

37. Install cabinets, cabinet trim, other storage units
38. Install countertops, back splashes
39. Install baseboards and remaining prepainted trim
40. Install sink and faucet
41. Install toilet
42. Finish tub and shower plumbing
43. Finish installing electrical fixtures
44. Install towel bars and other accessories
45. Install flooring if this has not been done
46. Clean up and remove trash
47. Touch up paint and stains
48. Test electrical and plumbing systems
49. Obtain final inspections
50. Move in

Once you have established the sequence of construction, estimate the time needed to complete each step. Transfer this information to a calendar or make the sequence list into a time line by writing in the starting and ending date for each job. Adjust the time line to coordinate it with the delivery of materials. This will give you an estimated time of completion and a set of milestones along the way by which to check your progress.

EXPERT ADVICE

If a supplier requires a deposit before ordering materials, have the receipt specify that the deposit is refundable if delivery is not met by a given date.

ASSESS YOUR ABILITIES

The following questions will help you assess your readiness for various levels of involvement. For best results, be truthful and answer each question fully.

MANAGING THE PROJECT

You may want to manage the job yourself and hire subcontractors to do the actual work. Although this entails hiring professionals, you will still have certain responsibilities.
■ Are you well organized, persistent, and clear about the details of your design?
■ Are you free to spend time on the telephone and at the job?
■ Can you handle money, make payments promptly, and keep a budget?
■ Are you comfortable negotiating with subcontractors and suppliers?
■ Are you articulate, firm, and patient?
■ Are you willing to be friendly but stay out of the way?
■ Are you able to direct all inquiries, complaints, or compliments to the person with whom you signed the contract—not to that person's employees?

Subcontractors depend on scheduling. If your job is not ready when they arrive, they will have to reschedule it, and you may not see them again for days. Keep subcontractors informed if you anticipate delays.

If you plan to hire salaried workers or unlicensed professionals who are not members of your own family, are you willing to take on the responsibilities of an employer? These responsibilities include reporting wages to the IRS, withholding state and federal taxes, paying the employer's share of those taxes, and carrying a Worker's Compensation insurance policy. Check your insurance to be sure you are adequately covered in this role.

PERFORMING A TRADE

You may want to perform one or more of the construction trades.
■ Are you experienced in a trade (such as carpentry or wiring) or with a material (such as wallboard, paint, or tile)?
■ Do you have access to the proper tools?
■ Are you willing to be assigned as subcontractor by the contractor, and can you make yourself available on demand, have your materials ready, and complete the work as scheduled?

If you answered "yes" to the above questions, you can cut costs by doing some jobs yourself. You could do the work of the most highly paid professionals (usually plumbers and electricians) if you have the skills. You could do the tasks that have a high labor cost relative to the materials cost, such as wallboard finishing, insulating, and painting. Any small jobs that would take a subcontractor less than half a day to perform, such as installing resilient sheet flooring, could also be done by you.

DOING GENERAL LABOR

You or members of your family may want to consider doing general labor on your project. General labor is a good entry level position into the construction grades. You may want to plan your project for the summer so high school or college students could participate.
■ Is there a significant amount of demolition, hauling, or simple alterations that you could do before the professionals take over?
■ Are you available on short notice to assist with menial tasks?
■ Can it be clearly specified in the contract which tasks are the contractor's responsibility and which are yours?
■ Are you in good physical condition?
■ Do you mind getting dirty?

DOING EVERYTHING YOURSELF

Doing the entire job yourself can be time consuming and frustrating, but it can also be highly satisfying.
■ Do you enjoy working on your home?
■ Do you have the time?
■ Will the project disrupt normal day-to-day living?
■ Will it matter if the project remains unfinished for several weeks?
■ Have your determined that the project will not entail removing lead paint or asbestos?
■ Have you finished every project you ever started?
■ Will other family members participate or support your doing everything yourself?

WORKING WITH THE PROS

Many types of professionals can help you design, build, or remodel your bathroom. Consult them early in the project when their expertise is most valuable.

DESIGN PROS

Architects are trained in structural planning and in the overall arrangement of space. Unless you expect to move major walls or make other substantial alterations, you probably won't need an architect.

Interior designers normally work with surfaces and finish materials, but many are qualified to help plan interior changes and can assist with other phases of the project.

Bathroom designers are specialists knowledgeable about bathroom products, trends, and developments. They may own an independent firm or may work for a dealer who sells bathroom fixtures and supplies. Some are designated as CBD, signifying membership in the Society of Certified Bathroom Designers, under the auspices of the National Kitchen and Bath Association. Membership is based on professional experience, training, and a qualifying examination.

Designers have different ways of structuring their fees. Some work for a fixed hourly rate. Some may charge a flat fee for designing the entire bathroom. Others may charge a percentage of the total construction cost or a percentage of the cost of certain fixtures and supplies.

CONSTRUCTION PROS

These are the people who get the job done. Each has specialized skills that your project may require.

■ GENERAL CONTRACTORS oversee construction and are responsible for completing the project as specified in the plans. Some contractors offer design services as well, thus handling the entire project. A general contractor hires the subcontractors and supervises their work.

■ PLUMBERS: Unless you are accomplished at home remodeling and repairs, you will need the expertise of a plumber to reroute pipes or to add new fixtures.

■ ELECTRICIANS rough in new wiring, add circuits, install wiring for a whirlpool, and install finish fixtures and outlets.

■ CARPENTERS are responsible for all woodworking, including repair or replacement of the subfloor and installation of finish trim.

Cabinetmakers build cabinets and storage units to specifications.

■ OTHERS: Depending on your design, you may need to contract with tile setters, glass block installers, wallpaper hangers, and other construction professionals. These specialists may be independent contractors or they may work for the suppliers of these products.

Although a license may be necessary to perform any of the above tasks in your state, other qualities—such as experience and recommendations of satisfied clients—are just as important.

HIRING CONTRACTORS

Finding the right contractor is just as important as choosing the right bathtub or estimating costs. The time-honored method of selection is through competitive bidding, but bathroom remodeling does not always lend itself to fixed bids because there are so many variables. Going with the lowest bid does not guarantee you will be satisfied with the quality of the service.

To reduce variables and make fixed-bid contracts go smoothly, be sure to:
■ Provide detailed plans and specifications
■ Distinguish clearly between your role and that of the contractor
■ Set clear terms for writing change orders

An alternative to the fixed-bid contract is the time-and-materials contract. The advantages of this type is that you pay only the actual cost of the job and you get more attentive service. The disadvantages are that you don't know exactly how much the job will cost until it is finished and you don't know what another contractor would charge to do the same job.

The main thing to recognize is that you are shopping for a unique service, not a product. If you solicit fixed bids, observe the following guidelines of etiquette:
■ Do not solicit a formal bid if you have a contractor in mind. Just negotiate directly.
■ In your initial phone call to each contractor, describe the project briefly and mention that complete plans are available.
■ Have ready a list of questions. Ask about the contractors' experience with similar projects and about their method of scheduling construction. Remember to ask for references.
■ Check references by visiting job sites and completed projects. Ask previous clients if they were satisfied with the contractor's performance and attitude.

■ Narrow your choices to three or four and provide a complete set of plans to each one.
■ Set a firm date for receiving bids. Allow at least two weeks if the project is a complete remodel involving several subcontractors.
■ Specify what materials and labor you intend to provide.
■ If a bidder requests clarification or further information, answer the request in writing. Send each bidder a copy of your answers, labeled "Addendum." Be sure to date it.
■ Use the same process to notify bidders of changes you make in the plans after they have been submitted for bids.
■ Along with the price quote, request bank or credit references and a copy of the contract form that the bidder expects you to sign.
■ Review all bids and forms carefully.

It is unethical to negotiate simultaneously with two contractors after you have received their bids, or to invite another contractor to compete after bidding has closed. Remember to notify all parties of your choice and of the winning bid price, and thank everyone for taking the time to bid.

SIGNING THE CONTRACT

Insist on a well-written contract. It does not have to be elaborate. A good contract should include these provisions, although not all of them will apply to every situation.
■ Reference to the construction documents as the criteria of performance
■ Stipulation that the contractor must obtain permits, perform work to code, and get necessary inspections
■ Specified start and completion dates and a detailed schedule
■ Clear delineation between the contractor's supervisory duties and your own
■ Specification of the work you intend to do yourself
■ List all materials or fixtures you will be supplying
■ Payment schedule corresponding to key completion dates
■ Stipulation that the contractor will provide lien releases from all

suppliers and subcontractors before final payment is made
■ Requirements for final payment, including final inspection by the building department, a certificate of completion signed by you and the architect, and a 30-day waiting period
■ Certificate of insurance from the contractor and subcontractors covering all risks and naming you as the beneficiary
■ A procedure for handling change orders
■ Specific procedures for communication when more than one professional is involved
■ A method for resolving disputes
■ Clear policies pertaining to on-the-job use of tobacco, radios, drugs, and alcohol

Complex bathrooms can be ambitious projects for most homeowners to tackle on their own. A room like this can involve a variety of contractors, including tile setters, framers, finish carpenters, and electricians.

UNDERSTANDING PERMITS

Most communities require a building permit before construction begins. For remodeling projects, the homeowner is usually allowed to apply for the permit, but in some communities permits may be issued only to licensed contractors.

The permit will probably be issued immediately if you are making only minor alterations to an existing bathroom. If you are making major structural changes, the building inspection department may be required to check the plans, a process that could take several days. Separate permits are customarily issued for the building, plumbing, electrical, and mechanical stages of the project.

You gain several advantages when you obtain a permit:
■ You have complied with the law.
■ The permit validates any work affecting resale value of the house.
■ It decreases the possibility of an insurance company refusing a claim against fire or other damages of dubious origin.
■ It gives you an incentive to plan the project thoroughly.
■ It instills a sense of pride in your work.
■ Codes exist to ensure that you and your family will be living in a safe home.

A large mirror makes this stylish bath seem bigger by reflecting images from across the room.

INSPECTIONS

The permit will include a schedule of inspections. Generally, all work must be inspected before it is covered up. A final inspection is made after everything is hooked up and ready to go. A typical schedule of inspections appears on page 53.

Your contractor will call for inspections and will be responsible for answering questions. However, you may have to arrange to let the inspector onto the premises if the contractor cannot be there.

The local building inspection department can tell you what codes pertain to your work and can answer specific questions about code requirements. However, staff members cannot tell you how to do the work. If you have done the work yourself and are not sure whether it will meet code, hire a professional who is familiar with the local codes to take a look at the job before the inspection.

PREPARING YOURSELF FOR CONSTRUCTION

A remodeling project inevitably causes disruptions and mess. Water turned off at the wrong time is annoying; the lack of a door, inconvenient; the loss of a bathroom for several days, nerve-wracking. The more familiar you are with the plans and the schedule, the better you will be able to cope. Prepare as much as possible ahead of time, before you have to move out of the bathroom.
- Clear out the work site.
- Plan how and where to pile debris.
- Collect cardboard boxes for carrying out plaster and scraps.
- Inquire about rental rates for a debris box or a truck.
- Place orders early for materials with long delivery times.
- Clear out the garage or some similar area where large bulky items (such as bathtub or shower stall) can be stored.
- Decide what to do with old fixtures.
- Prepare family members for disruption.
- Consider avoidance: This might be a good time for the kids to spend a weekend with their grandparents or friends.
- If you'll be involved in the work, be sure you're up to the task physically. Don't plan long days of hard work if you're out of shape.
- Assess the condition of your tools, too. Buy the things you need before the work begins.
- Above all, maintain a sense of humor.

TOOL BOX

If you plan to do some of the construction yourself, inventory your tools and organize them for quick access. It will make the job go more smoothly.
- Replace broken tools; sharpen dull ones
- Mark tools if there will be other people working at the site
- Buy safety goggles, gloves, dust masks
- Check ladders and power cords for safety
- Provide a First Aid kit and a heavy shop-type vacuum cleaner.

When construction is under way, be sure to schedule breaks when you can get away from the project. If a supplier requires a deposit before ordering materials, have the receipt specify that the deposit is refundable if delivery is not met by a given date.

INSPECTION SCHEDULE

Job	Work to Be Checked	Time of Inspection
Foundation	Trench, forms, rebar	Before concrete is poured
Under floor	Floor framing, utility lines	Before subfloor is installed
Framing	Grade and size of lumber, spans, connections, sheathing	Before walls are insulated or covered
Rough plumbing	Pipe sizes, fittings, pressure test	Before framing is inspected or walls are covered
Rough wiring	Wire size, boxes, bends	Before framing is inspected or walls are covered
Rough mechanical	Ducts, flues, clearances, gas lines	Before framing is inspected or walls are covered
Insulation	Thickness, joints, cracks	Before wallboard is applied
Interior walls	Wallboard nailing pattern (may not be required)	Before joints are taped
Final inspection	Electrical fixtures, plumbing fixtures, window glass, stairs	After completion

54

CONSTRUCTION GUIDE

Hands-on remodeling of a bathroom will challenge your abilities. The work requires careful preparation, close coordination, accuracy, and a variety of skills. It will probably mean having to get along without the bathroom for a few days—possibly even weeks. For most homeowners, however, the rewards of a beautiful, new bathroom and the satisfaction of having improved their home offset the inconvenience.

Whether you're doing all the construction yourself, hiring a contractor to do it, or dividing the task with construction professionals, this chapter will guide you through each phase, from demolition through finishing techniques. Tasks unique to bathroom remodeling—such as removing a bathtub and installing a toilet— are presented in complete step-by-step detail. Tasks common to all types of remodeling—such as framing walls, installing electrical wiring, and finishing plasterboard—are summarized briefly.

For a classic look that ages well, choose white fixtures. You can always alter the decor by changing the colors of the walls and accents. Be careful if you're considering a built-in step for the tub, as shown. It can be a safety concern, especially when wet.

PREPARING FOR CONSTRUCTION

Thoughtful preparation makes work go more easily after construction begins. First, arrange for the use of a bathroom while yours is out of commission. If you're fortunate enough to have a second bathroom, you'll suffer only minor inconvenience. If you're remodeling the only bathroom in the house, you have three options:

(1) Try to phase the project so at least the toilet and possibly the bathtub will be functional most of the time. If you are hiring professionals to do all the work, this approach may be more expensive, and you will probably have access to the bathroom only in the mornings and evenings.

(2) Rent or borrow facilities. Consider renting a portable toilet or a recreational vehicle with a bathroom for the duration of the project or rely on neighbors, friends, or family for the use of their bathroom.

(3) Take a vacation while your bathroom is being remodeled. The drawback to this option is you won't be at home to answer questions that inevitably come up during construction.

SAFETY

Think safety first at any construction site. Safe work habits, a minimum of clutter, basic safety equipment, and an awareness of your own limitations will greatly reduce your chances of being injured.

■ Have gloves, safety goggles, dust masks, and a hard hat available at all times, and use them whenever the situation calls for it.

■ Get a tetanus shot if you have not had one in the past 10 years.

■ Don't overdo physically; let your tools do the work.

■ Before tossing boards on the debris pile, always remove nails or bend them flat.

■ Wear a particle mask or a respirator during dusty operations.

■ If you encounter asbestos (rare in the bathroom except in some flooring materials), seek professional assistance.

■ Read directions carefully for solvents, adhesives, and other flammable products.

■ Avoid working when you are physically or mentally fatigued and be extra alert toward the end of the day.

■ Use power tools with care. Make sure the safety guards are intact. Wear goggles. Do not wear loose clothing. Be sure electrical cords and tools are in good condition and are properly grounded. Keep saw blades and drill bits sharp.

■ Turn off circuit breakers or disconnect fuses serving the wires where you will be working. Cover the breaker with tape to warn other people it was turned off intentionally. Use a voltage tester to double-check all wires in electrical outlets or fixtures you plan to work on. When in doubt, consult an electrician.

It is not likely you will be working on gas appliances or encountering gas lines in a bathroom. However, if you inadvertently disconnect a gas line, be prepared to shut off the main gas valve immediately. It's a good idea to have a service representative from the utility company come out and help when you're ready to turn the gas back on and to relight the pilots.

TOOL BOX

Construction goes much more smoothly when you have the right tools. Most tasks can be done with basic hand tools, but be sure they are good quality. Don't hesitate to buy a tool you don't have. There is no substitute for the right equipment. Depending on the scope of the work, you will need:

■ A hammer with a ripping claw
■ A utility knife with extra blades
■ A flat pry bar
■ A demolition or cold chisel
■ A 3-inch-wide putty knife
■ A mini-hacksaw
■ A small handsaw
■ An adjustable wrench
■ Adjustable pliers
■ Pipe wrenches
■ An assortment of screwdrivers
■ A framing square
■ A simple voltage tester

More specialized tools include:

■ Needle-nose pliers
■ Side cutters
■ End cutters
■ A large crowbar
■ A brickset
■ A basin wrench
■ A sledgehammer
■ A maul
■ A flat shovel for loading debris

Helpful power tools include:

■ A reciprocating saw with both long and short blades
■ A ⅜-inch drill with screwdriver bits (cordless if you are buying a new one)
■ A circular saw with carbide tipped blades

LOGISTICS

Decide beforehand how you will deal with debris and where to store materials. Even a modest bathroom project can generate a mountain of trash. You can haul everything away as you remove it (which requires a pickup truck, trailer, or large station wagon); you can pile the debris in an inconspicuous but convenient spot and have it hauled away at the end of the job; or you can rent a debris box and toss trash into it as you go. Most debris box services require pickup within a week. So you can save money and stay on good terms with your neighbors if you complete the demolition within that time.

Make arrangements for storing fixtures or cabinets you plan to reuse, as well as new materials which may be delivered before you need them. Some materials can be stored outside under a tarp, but others (such as cabinets and wallboard) must be stored in a dry, covered area. A large garage with easy driveway access or an empty room inside the house is ideal. Also, designate a convenient and well-organized area for storing tools.

CONSTRUCTION TIP

Constructing a new bathroom or remodeling an existing one requires the same expertise. Remodeling, however, adds steps to the building process. Allow plenty of time to demolish or remove existing fixtures before beginning new construction.

Formerly a small 6×8-foot space, this master bath was visually enlarged by opening the ceiling to the roof and adding skylights for more light. An adjacent guest bedroom sacrificed space for a roomy new shower.

DEMOLITION

It's easy to think of demolition as sledgehammer work, but seldom does it require brute strength.

You'll be more successful if you think of it as finesse work, taking things a step at a time and chipping away at the bathroom rather than trying to demolish everything at once.

Even if you're moving walls or making structural changes, demolition requires more common sense than technical skill and knowledge of a few fundamentals rather than an answer to every question. Planning the job carefully, using the proper tools, and developing safe work habits will do more to ensure a successful project than simply having the appropriate skills and techniques.

This powder room has a nautical air. Sea charts become intriguing wallpaper on one wall. Another wall resembles a planked hull, and the mirror mimics a porthole.

WARM-UP EXERCISES

■ Before beginning work, seal off all doorways and passages to keep dust and debris out of the rest of the house. Shut any doors that can be left closed. Apply duct tape all around the edges, especially around the bottom, sticking the tape to the door and to the floor. For doors that must remain in use, apply duct tape along the bottom on both sides, sticking it to the door but not to the floor. That way the tape acts as a dust sweep as you open and close the door. Passageways without doors can be sealed with 4-mil plastic sheeting and duct tape.
■ Temporarily mount an exhaust fan in a bathroom window to eliminate dust.
■ With the bathroom sealed off from the rest of the house, lay a trail of drop cloths or sheets of cardboard between the bathroom and the outdoors, and between the bathroom door and adjacent rooms. This helps protect the landscaping, as well as the floors in other parts of the house.
■ Remove all the little accessories, including towel bars, soap dish, toothbrush holder, light fixtures, and window treatments. Be especially careful with anything you intend to save; find a space well away from the construction site

to store these things. Next, remove the easiest and least necessary items; these are usually the ones that do not involve plumbing. Remove the plumbing fixtures last. You might even wait to take out the fixtures when the new units are ready to install, especially if you will be using the bathroom during remodeling.

REMOVING SHELVES AND STORAGE UNITS

Shelving units are relatively easy to dismantle. Detach them from the wall, either by unscrewing their fasteners or by gently prying them from the wall with a flat bar. If the shelf is sealed to the wall with layers of paint, use a utility knife to score through the seal. If you intend to save the wall, place a flat shim, such as a piece of ½-inch plywood, between the wall and the pry bar to prevent gouging.

Some bathrooms have prefabricated storage, much like kitchen cabinets, that can be removed in one piece and saved. Open the unit and look for screws on the back panel where it's attached to the wall. Unscrew them and remove the cabinet. Storage cabinets in most older bathrooms were built in place and must be dismantled. Start by taking out the drawers, doors, and shelves. Try to determine how the unit was constructed and work backwards, removing first the pieces that were installed last. Knock each piece loose with a hammer, pry it out, or cut it off with a saw.

To remove a surface-mounted medicine cabinet, start by scoring around the edge to break the paint seal. Look inside for the screws holding the cabinet to the wall. The screws may be covered with paint, so look for telltale depressions near each corner. Scrape off the paint and unscrew them. The cabinet should come loose. If it is secured with nails, gently pry the whole cabinet from the wall or pull the nails from the inside with a cat's paw and a hammer.

A flush-mounted medicine cabinet is usually held in place on two sides with screws. Remove the screws and pull the cabinet out of the wall cavity. Old wood cabinets may have to be dismantled piece by piece, starting with the door.

REMOVING SINKS

Sinks may be wall mounted, freestanding, or set into a countertop. Removal is similar for all three types. The task usually can be done by one person, although you may need help to remove a wall-mounted cast-iron sink.

Turn off the water supply at the shutoff valves below the sink. In rare cases where there are no shutoff valves, turn water off at the main house valve. Leave the faucet in the sink and remove them as one unit. You can detach the faucet later if you intend to reuse it or the sink. Have a bucket or pan handy that will fit under the shutoff valves and the P-trap.

DISCONNECT PLUMBING: Place the bucket or dishpan under the shutoff valves and disconnect the water supply lines (the vertical tubes) with an adjustable wrench. Open the sink faucet to allow any water trapped in the lines to drain into the bucket. If there are no shutoff valves, disconnect the water pipes from the faucet. Use a basin wrench to reach underneath the sink and unscrew the connecting nuts, or use a hacksaw to cut through the old pipes. You will want to replace them and install proper shutoff valves. Place a bucket under the P-trap and loosen the slip nuts with a pair of slip-joint pliers. Finish unscrewing them by hand and drop the trap into the bucket.

REMOVE WALL-MOUNTED LAVATORY: Look underneath for the bolts or screws securing it to the mounting bracket. Remove them. With a helper, lift the sink straight up

until it clears the mounting bracket. Set the sink aside and remove screws holding the mounting bracket to the wall. Take off the mounting bracket.

PEDESTAL SINKS: There are two types.
■ The first is simply a wall-mounted sink with a pedestal placed under it for decoration. Look for any bolts or screws securing the pedestal to the floor and remove them. Carefully slide out the pedestal and remove the sink in the same way as any other wall-mounted model.
■ The second type is completely supported by the pedestal, so remove the sink first (there may be screws or bolts holding it to the wall and to the pedestal) then the pedestal.

COUNTERTOP STYLES: A sink set into a countertop can be removed separately or along with the counter. If you remove it separately, the technique you use will depend on whether the rim is mounted above or below the surface of the counter.
■ The simplest installation is a basin with an integral rim resting on the countertop. Pry under the rim with a flat bar to loosen it and then lift out the basin.
■ In a similar but more complicated installation, a surface-mounted metal rim holds the sink in place with clips installed from below. Loosen the clips with a screwdriver and remove them. The basin will drop as soon as you do this, so if it is heavy or fragile, secure it first with a rope and 2×4s.
■ If countertop material covers the rim of the sink, or if it is installed flush with the rim, you will have to remove the countertop before you take out the sink. If it is a tile counter, use a hammer and chisel to chip away the trim pieces locking the basin rim in place. Wear gloves and goggles to protect yourself. If the countertop is a solid slab of cultured marble or similar material, remove it in one piece before taking out the sink.

REMOVING COUNTERTOPS AND VANITIES

■ Remove doors and drawers from the vanity. Then look inside for the fastening brackets, screws, or other devices holding the countertop in place. Unscrew them and remove the countertop. Some slab counters are attached to the vanity only by a bead of caulk. Working from above, slide a putty knife or scraper between the slab and the vanity to break the seal. This prevents the slab from snapping when you pry it off. Pry the countertop loose around the edges with a flat bar and lift it away.

DEMOLITION
continued

■ Tile countertops may have a plywood base that was attached to the vanity from above before tile was installed. This base cannot be reached without demolishing the tile. To avoid this, try to remove the countertop in one piece by prying it up and away from the vanity—or remove the vanity with the countertop still attached.

■ Remove any screws holding the vanity to the wall. They are usually located along the top rail. Slide the vanity forward, lifting it clear of the flooring, and carry it away.

REMOVING TOILETS

Taking out a toilet is quite simple, even for someone working alone. The hardest part is lifting out the fixture and carrying it away.

■ If you are salvaging the toilet or the toilet seat, remove the seat and lid by unscrewing the nuts that hold them in place. Turn off the water supply to the toilet and remove the tank lid. Flush the toilet until both the bowl and the tank are empty, and sponge up any remaining water.

■ Disconnect the water supply line by unscrewing the retaining nut at the bottom of the tank or the coupling nut at the shutoff valve. Unscrew both if you wish to remove the supply tubing. Cover the exposed outlet of the shutoff valve with tape to prevent dust and debris from falling in. To make it easier to lift out the bowl, first remove the tank. Unscrew the two or three nuts holding the tank to the bowl and lift it off. Some old toilets have a wall-mounted tank connected to the bowl by an L-shaped pipe. Remove the pipe first by unscrewing the coupling nuts and any retaining bolts. Remove the bolts holding the tank to the wall and set the tank aside.

■ To remove the bowl, pry off the plastic or ceramic caps covering the closet bolts and remove the nuts with a small wrench. Rock the bowl gently back and forth to loosen it from the wax seal around the drain flange. Lift it carefully. A considerable amount of water will be left in the drain trap. Set the toilet in the tub or shower and tip it to drain this water out before carrying the toilet through the house. (Place old towels in the bottom of the tub or shower to keep the toilet from scratching it.)

■ Temporarily seal the drainpipe opening with rags, duct tape, or an expansion plug to keep debris out and to keep sewer gas from entering the house.

■ Slide the closet bolts out of the slots in the exposed drain flange and scrape away the old wax seal with a putty knife. If you intend to install a new toilet in the same place, inspect the flange for cracks or other damage and replace it if necessary.

FLOOR COVERINGS

It is not always necessary to remove the old floor covering in order to install a new one. However, you must remove it if the subfloor is damaged and needs to be repaired. If the old floor covering is linoleum or vinyl that is in good condition and free of wax or polish, many kinds of flooring can be laid directly over it. If it is cracked and uneven, you may be able to patch it; otherwise install a plywood or hardboard underlayment over it and install the new floor on top of that. New tile may require a structural underlayment to stiffen the floor.

The old flooring should be removed if laying new flooring over it will raise the level too high. This can happen if there is more than one layer of flooring, if the finish floor is installed over an underlayment, or if tile was installed over a mortar bed. Old flooring should also be removed if the new flooring or underlayment will not adhere to it.

■ To remove the old floor covering, begin by prying off any baseboards covering it at the edges. If you expect to reuse the baseboard, score the joint between it and the wall with a utility knife to break the paint seal. Pry off the baseboard gently. If it resists, drive the finishing nails completely through it with a nail set and lift it free. If any nails are left in the baseboard after you remove it, pull them out with pliers. Work from the back so as not to mar the finished surface. To remove rubber or vinyl base coving, run a 3-inch-wide putty knife behind it and gently pry it loose.

ASBESTOS CAUTION

The backing on some older linoleum and tiles contains asbestos fibers that are released into the air when the flooring is broken or jarred. If your flooring is old linoleum or vinyl, don't sand it! Before proceeding with demolition, call a local environmental agency and have the material tested. Officials there will tell you what precautions to take and what legal requirements you must meet. At the least, wear safety goggles, gloves, and a respirator designated for asbestos when you remove it, and dispose of the pieces in airtight plastic bags. Depending on the type of material, it may be necessary to have the flooring removed by a licensed asbestos contractor.

Storage makes this bathroom practical. Repeated forms make it stylish. Notice the arch of the window echoed by the mirror, the recurring columns, and patterns in the tile.

DEMOLITION
continued

Compartmentalizing makes this bathroom comfortable for family use. Glass, mirrors, and reflective tile keep it bright. The selection of colorful towels allows practical storage to be decorative, as well.

■ Remove linoleum or vinyl tiles by prying them up, one by one, using a wide pry bar, a putty knife, a chisel, or a floor scraper. Sometimes they will pop right out. Usually the mastic is strong, and you are in for a tedious, time-consuming job. Take precautions if you need to remove older tile that may contain asbestos fibers (*see Asbestos Caution on page 60*).

■ Remove sheet vinyl or linoleum following the procedures outlined above. The job will be easier if you first slice the flooring into small sections with a utility knife. Pry up the sections and scrape off any mastic remaining on the floor.

■ Resilient flooring, whether sheet or tile, may have been installed over an underlayment of plywood, hardboard, or similar material. If so, it is much easier to pull up the underlayment and flooring together than it is to remove just the flooring. First cut the underlayment into sections 3 or 4 feet square. Use a circular saw with an old carbide blade (you will probably hit nails) and set the blade depth so it will just cut through the underlayment without cutting into the subfloor. Pry up the sections of underlayment and flooring together and discard them.

■ Remove ceramic tile with a hammer and a wide chisel. A brickset works well. To remove the first tile, break it into pieces and chip them out. Force the chisel underneath the adjacent whole tiles and pop them up. Wear gloves and goggles.

If the tile floor was installed over a mortar bed, it's usually easier to force up the mortar than it is to remove the individual tiles. Use a large crowbar or a pickax to pry underneath the mortar bed. Alternately lift on the bar and hammer down next to it with a sledgehammer. When the bed cracks, it may expose reinforcing wires. Cut them with wire cutters and remove each section. Work carefully to avoid injuring yourself or damaging the subfloor. In most cases, an old mortar bed extends down between the floor joists where it is supported by boards laid over cleats nailed to the sides of the joists. Sometimes the joists have been tapered at the top, in which case you must attach 2×4 nailers on both sides of each joist, flush with the top, to support a new subfloor.

It is sometimes possible to install resilient sheet flooring over ceramic tile. The tile must be in good condition. Roughen it first by sanding it with coarse abrasive paper. Attach a plywood underlayment to the tile, using construction glue and a caulking gun.

REMOVING LIGHTS AND ELECTRICAL FIXTURES

You can either remove lights and other fixtures during the demolition process or when rough wiring is being installed. It depends on what other work is being done.

You will need to remove the lights if you are removing wall or ceiling materials around them, if you are changing their location, or if you are doing extensive rewiring. If you are simply replacing lights, do not remove the old ones until you are ready to install new ones.

■ Most bathroom light fixtures are surface-mounted ceiling or wall units with some kind of globe. Remove the globe and the light bulb. Loosen the screws holding the housing to the electrical box inside the wall or ceiling. Gently pull the housing out far enough to expose the wiring. Disconnect the fixture wires from the house wires and remove the fixture. Cap the house wires with wire nuts and push them back into the electrical box.

■ To remove a fluorescent fixture, first take out the tube. Then, loosen the screws or nuts holding the cover in place and lift it away to expose the wires. Disconnect the fixture wires from the house wires, unless the connection is made inside the electrical box. In that case, remove the fixture housing by loosening the circular locknut from the hollow stud the wires go through; pull the housing away from the wall or ceiling; and disconnect the wires. Cap the house wires and push them back into the electrical box.

■ Remove all covers from the electrical outlets and switches. This will make it easier to demolish the wall and ceiling materials. The fixtures themselves can be left in place until they are moved or replaced when installing new wiring.

REMOVING WALL AND CEILING MATERIALS

It may not be necessary to take out any wall or ceiling materials. You may be able to paint or wallpaper the old surfaces. However, if the walls and ceiling are in poor shape, or if you intend to alter the structure, the wiring, or the plumbing, then some surface materials must be removed. If you are only providing access for small changes in the plumbing and wiring, you can wait until later to make the openings—but be prepared for surprises.

Removing wall and ceiling materials can be messy and time-consuming, but it is not particularly complicated. Wear gloves, goggles, a dust mask, and a hard hat when you are removing plaster or plasterboard. Turn off

SAFETY TIP

To remove any kind of electrical fixture, first turn off the circuit breakers for the bathroom area and put tape over the handles so no one turns them back on.

DEMOLITION
continued

the electrical circuits near the walls you are working on, and work carefully to avoid hitting wires, pipes, or ducts. If the project is a renovation with extensive structural, wiring, and plumbing alterations, gut the room to the wall studs and ceiling framing. It is tempting to leave small sections of wall or ceiling

There's no turning back once you've pulled out fixtures and torn into walls. An exhaust fan in the window will reduce the plaster dust that seems to drift everywhere.

intact, but they are seldom worth saving—it is tedious to patch into them, and you will probably need to get behind them to work on the wiring or insulation.

TRIM: Remove trim first. If you plan to save it, score along the edge of each piece with a utility knife. Pry it off the wall with a flat bar and pull the nails out through the back with a pair of end cutters. Mark each piece so you will know later where it goes.

CERAMIC TILE: Remove wall tiles as you would remove floor tiles (*see page 61*).

WALLCOVERINGS: To remove a single layer of wallcovering, spray it with wallpaper remover, one section at a time. Let the solution set, respray, and peel off each section with a wide putty knife. Start from the floor and work upward at an angle. To remove several layers, rent a steamer or hire professional help.

After the wallcovering is off, wash down the wall with a sponge and a weak solution of trisodium phosphate (TSP). Rinse and let dry. Sand any uneven areas.

PLASTERBOARD: Cut a clean line all around the section you intend to remove. If this section includes a corner, cut through the joint tape with a utility knife. If demolition is to stop in the middle of a wall or ceiling, make the cut down the center of a stud or joist. Use a hammer and chisel, a sharp utility knife, or a circular saw set to the depth of the plasterboard. Sawing will cause a lot of dust; chiseling or scoring is more tedious but cleaner. Now is the time to use that exhaust fan you rigged in the window.

Tear the plasterboard off the framing in large chunks, using a ripping hammer, a wrecking bar, or your hands. Always pull; never push. Wear gloves, a dust mask, and goggles. Wear a hard hat if you're tearing out the ceiling; dust and insulation will come cascading down. Watch out for wires hidden behind the walls. Pull the nails as you go.

To remove a small section of plasterboard, lay out the guidelines with a framing square. The top and bottom lines should be level. The side lines should be centered over studs. To mark the studs, knock a small hole in the center of the proposed opening and insert a tape measure through the hole, horizontally, until the end reaches a stud. Transfer this measurement to the surface of the wall, add ¾ inch (half the thickness of the stud), and make a mark on the wall. This mark indicates the center of the stud. Repeat the operation for the stud on the other side. To cut, use a drywall saw or a reciprocating saw between the studs and make repeated passes with a utility knife where the line passes over a stud.

LATH AND PLASTER: Use a hammer and chisel to score a break line at the point where the demolition will end. Tap gently but firmly. Strip the plaster from the lath with the claw of a ripping hammer or a wrecking bar. Then remove the lath a piece at a time. If the end of a lath is locked into a corner, rock it up and down, not side to side, to work it free.

Making smaller openings requires careful work to avoid jarring loose the adjacent plaster. First lay out guidelines. Center them over studs (to find the studs, probe with a hammer and nail). Cut along the lines with a hammer and chisel and remove the plaster.

Use a hammer and a sharp chisel to cut through the lath where it crosses the studs. If you are cutting lath between the studs, use a keyhole saw, bearing heavily on the push stroke and lightly on the pull stroke. It is also messy but possible to cut through lath and plaster with a circular saw. Use a carbide-tipped blade set to the depth of the lath and run the saw firmly and slowly. Loose lath can bind the blade, so be ready for kickbacks.

REMOVING SHOWER STALLS

Whether you plan to refurbish the existing shower stall or remove it completely, it should be gutted all the way down to the studs. You may want to leave the shower pan in place if it is in good condition and if it harmonizes with the new tile. Otherwise, take it out, too.

■ Remove the shower door by unscrewing the hinges or the channel supporting it. Then dismantle the frame. Some pieces may be held in place by screws, others by caulk or putty. These can be pried out or knocked free.

■ Remove faucet handles and showerhead.

■ Remove the wallcovering. If the stall is a plastic or fiberglass unit, remove enough plasterboard to expose the flanges around the top. Remove the nails holding the flanges in place and pry out the stall in sections. Wear gloves and goggles. If you wish to remove the stall in one piece, disconnect the drain first.

To remove a tile surround (especially one set in a mortar bed), take special precautions. Tile and mortar are heavy, and broken tile is sharp. Wear thick clothing, gloves, goggles, a hard hat, and heavy shoes. Protect fixtures (if you are saving them) with thick tarps, layers of cardboard, or plywood. Remove the tile and mortar in sections. Start at the bottom of each section and work up. Use a chisel and a maul to break the tile and mortar into pieces and a crowbar to pry pieces off the wall.

■ To disconnect the drain on a prefabricated unit, remove the drain cover and look for a ring or other fastening device around the edge of the drain. Unscrew and remove it, along with any gaskets. Lift the shower pan to clear the floor pipe, then pull it out.

■ A tiled shower pan is more difficult to remove because it is set in a mortar bed and must be broken up. Remove any framing supporting the curb. This will expose some of the mortar bed. Break away as much of it as you can, then pry underneath the mortar bed with a large crowbar to break up the pan. Leave the drain intact until you've removed all mortar and tile. The drain should be replaced if you are installing a new shower in the same location. Otherwise, remove it by sawing through the pipe just below floor level. Cap the open pipe to block sewer gas.

■ If you are removing the stall completely, take out the water pipes. Turn off the water at the main valve and drain the pipes. To do this, first open any faucets in the house that are at a lower level than the shower pipes and then open the shower valve. Using a hacksaw and pipe wrenches, remove the pipes back to out-of-the-way fittings that you can cap.

■ Remove studs and framing members of the partition walls. Cut through studs at an angle so as not to bind the saw.

REMOVING BATHTUBS

The bathtub is the hardest of all bathroom fixtures to remove. For that reason, it is usually saved until last. It is large and heavy, and the plumbing may be hard to reach. If the tub is a freestanding claw-foot model, you can probably get to the plumbing quite easily. However, if the tub is built into an alcove or corner, you will need to gain access to the back of the plumbing wall. You also will need to remove tile or trim around the rim. In any case, you will need at least two helpers.

■ Remove the shower doors and their frame, if installed. Some doors can be removed simply by lifting them off the tracks. To remove others, you must raise the top bar slightly while a helper lifts each door out of the bottom track. When the doors are out, lift the top bar completely free of the frame. Remove side and bottom bars by unscrewing them or by prying them loose.

■ Turn off the water to the tub. Some bathtubs have shutoff valves located behind a door or a removable panel on the backside of the end wall. If there are no shutoff valves, turn off the water at the main valve.

■ If there is no removable panel behind the end wall, cut an opening to provide access to the drainpipes. Cut so that the sides are centered over studs, the bottom is about 2 inches above the floor or the baseboard, and the top is slightly above the rim of the tub. (To cut, use the techniques outlined on pages 62–63.)

■ Disconnect the drain by unscrewing the coupling nut at the top of the P-trap. With the nut loosened, the tub drainpipe should separate from the P-trap when the tub is lifted slightly, making it unnecessary to remove the entire drain and overflow assembly. Remove the drain and overflow assembly if you are unable to lift the tub or if the assembly will get in the way as you slide the tub out. Disassemble the overflow cover and the stopper mechanism, and take them out. Remove the screws holding the overflow pipe in place.

■ Working from behind the tub, loosen the coupling nuts holding the overflow pipe and the drain elbow in place. The overflow pipe should come out. If you have to remove the drain elbow, work from inside the tub. Insert a drain wrench—a tool resembling a fork—into the crosspiece of the drain and unscrew it, using a screwdriver or heavy-duty pliers to twist the tool. (If you do not have this tool, try using the handle of a pair of pliers.) If the fitting resists, wait until the tub is out, then use a wrench to grip the bottom side of the fitting at the same time as you twist the top side.

■ Remove the faucet handles and spout. If the tub is a freestanding model, disconnect the water supply lines from the faucet and remove the tub. You will need helpers and a dolly.

■ For a built-in tub, remove enough of the wallcovering to expose the top of the rim (use the techniques described on page 63). If the tub has flanges anchored to the wall, remove them.

■ Using a pry bar and working with several helpers, raise one end of the tub until you can slide a lumber runner beneath it. Do the same thing with the other end. Slide the tub out of the alcove, set it on a dolly, and remove it. If it won't go through the doorway, take off the door. If it still won't clear, stand the tub on end and work it through the doorway narrow side first. Lower it onto the dolly when you get it outside the room. If you don't have a dolly, you can move a heavy tub on several short rollers cut from 1½-inch plastic drainpipe. Have plenty of help.

Some tubs may be too large or too heavy to take out. Break up a cast-iron tub with a sledgehammer and remove it in pieces. Cut a steel tub in half, using a reciprocating saw with a hacksaw blade.

MAKING STRUCTURAL IMPROVEMENTS

After demolition, it's time to prepare the space for new fixtures. This may involve anything from minor patching and to major structural, plumbing, electrical, and insulation work. It is beyond the scope of this book to cover everything involved, but some procedures are especially relevant.

Sequence of construction varies from project to project. One option is to finish the walls and floor before installing any fixtures. Another is to install all fixtures except the toilet, then lay the flooring, install the toilet, and finally paint the room. The order depends on the extent of the project, the materials involved, and the schedules of the people doing the work. You may need to flip back and forth through this chapter to create your own step-by-step plan.

This black-and-white bathroom highlights the lush colors of a golf course outside. A tall mirror doubles the view.

If the project involves adding a room, the shell can be framed and closed in before opening up the wall and disrupting the original bathroom. However, if any plumbing, wiring, or duct work will be routed under the new floor, it must be installed and inspected before you put in subflooring. You may have to alter bathroom plumbing to make the connections. Plumbing vents, chimneys, flues, and ventilating ducts that penetrate the roof should be installed before the roofing so they can be properly flashed. You may need to leave an opening in the exterior wall for removing old fixtures and debris and for delivering bulky items.

Rough framing techniques for a bathroom are the same as those for any other room and are summarized in the following guidelines. Start with repairs to the floor framing and subfloor.

FLOORS

A sound floor system is the first prerequisite for a successful remodeling project. Depending on the scope of your job, you may need to do only simple repairs or you may need to reinforce the entire floor. In most cases, you will want to put a new plywood subfloor over the whole bathroom. Use a subfloor glue and screws to hold the plywood firmly.

REPAIRS: The key to a good installation is preparation of the subsurface. First, inspect the subfloor and the floor framing. Look for rot damage, structural weaknesses, and surface deformities. If you have removed the old finish floor, you can inspect the subfloor from above, but any structural damage to the framing may go unnoticed unless you also inspect from below.

Pay close attention to the toilet and tub areas even if it means making inspection holes in a downstairs ceiling. If you

find damage, repair it now, whether the flooring is installed now or later.

Subflooring that is rotted or badly damaged should be replaced. Cut out a rectangular section of subfloor around the damaged area. The cutout should extend at least 12 inches beyond any rotted wood, and the edges should be centered over floor joists. Use a circular saw with the blade set to the depth of the subflooring so you won't cut any joists. Cut a replacement patch out of plywood of the same thickness as the subfloor. Allow 1/16–1/8 inch of clearance for expansion. Nail 2×4 blocking between the joists to support the edges of the patch. Set the patch in place and nail it to the joists and blocking with 8d ring-shank nails.

Floor joists and other framing members seldom need to be repaired unless the floor is sagging or decaying. Extensive structural repair will require professional help. If damage is limited to one or two joists, nail a length of lumber of the same width next to the damaged joist. Attach it with 12d or 16d common nails along the top edge, along the bottom edge, and down the center.

If the damage is due to rot, support both sides of the rotted section with temporary shoring and cut the section out. Nail a new joist to the truncated joist. The new joist should be long enough to rest on the girders or other bearing members. If this is not possible, it should extend at least 4 feet in each direction beyond the cutout. Nail the joists together with 12d or 16d common nails.

REINFORCEMENT: Bathtubs, particularly large luxury tubs or cast-iron models, can be extremely heavy. Ideally, the tub should be located over or near a foundation wall, a girder, or a bearing wall.

A tub that lies perpendicular to the joists (supported by several of them) is unlikely to exceed the capacity of joists that are sized for normal loads, not weakened by notches or holes, and supported by the foundation or bearing walls.

If the tub lies parallel to the joists or if it lies perpendicular to them but is centered over a long joist span, double up the joists under the tub's feet or edges.

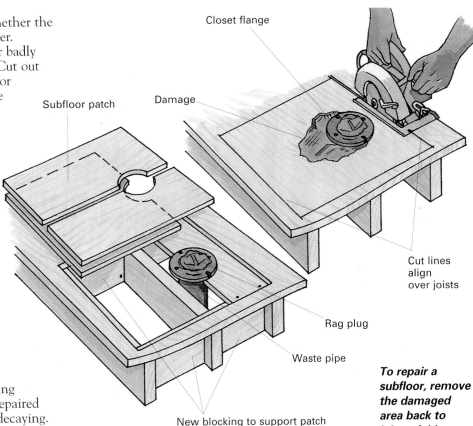

Closet flange

Subfloor patch

Damage

Cut lines align over joists

Rag plug

Waste pipe

New blocking to support patch

To repair a subfloor, remove the damaged area back to joists. Add blocking to uphold the repair, then fit a piece that you have cut to match the damaged segment.

CONSTRUCTION TIP

Before installing a new floor, check the condition of the subfloor and the supporting joists. Decayed subflooring, especially around the toilet and tub, is a common problem in older houses.

A sunken bathtub requires different floor support altogether. If the bathroom is located over a shallow crawl space, the tub should be supported by a concrete slab on the ground. If the bathroom is located over a basement or a first floor, the tub should be supported by dropped floor joists carried on bearing walls.

TOILET: The toilet in an upstairs bathroom may need special floor framing to provide enough room for the plumbing. If a joist is in the way, cut it and support it with headers. Double the headers and the joists supporting them if you have to cut more than one joist.

MAKING STRUCTURAL IMPROVEMENTS
continued

WALLS AND CEILINGS

When it comes to framing the ceiling and walls, certain details occur more often in bathrooms than in other rooms.

PLUMBING WALLS: Some plumbing cannot fit inside a 2×4 wall. To make an existing wall wide enough to accommodate plumbing, fur it out with 2×2s. If you are building a new wall, use 2×6 or 2×8 lumber.

WING WALLS: Partition walls (called wing walls or pony walls) jut out 2–3 feet from another wall. They often enclose a bathtub, create a toilet compartment, or define the end of a vanity cabinet. If they extend all the way from floor to ceiling, wing walls can be framed like any stud wall, with the top plates tied into the ceiling joists or into blocking set between the joists.

Many wing walls stop short of the ceiling, creating a feeling of space and admitting more natural light into an alcove. Because this type of wall has no support along the top and one edge, other means must be used to stabilize it. A well-secured cabinet, shelving, or counter installed against the wing wall and the adjacent wall can provide adequate support. If the wing wall is freestanding, there are several ways to increase its stability:

■ Assemble the framing with screws instead of nails.

■ Use ⅝- rather than ½-inch plasterboard or plywood (the plasterboard should be a water-resistant variety called wafer board or green board). And use glue to tighten its grip on the frame.

■ Anchor the front edge of the wall by using a long 2×4 for the last stud, extending it through the floor and attaching it to a joist or other framing underneath. This is particularly effective for walls that are subject to heavy traffic or that support extensive tiling.

SOFFITS: A soffit is a boxlike structure that creates a lower ceiling over features such as a vanity or a bathtub, or that fills in the space between the top of the wall cabinets and the ceiling. It is constructed on a simple ladder frame covered with plasterboard.

Frame the soffit with 2×2s to make it easier to drive nails or screws in both directions. Choose perfectly straight lumber—any warps or bows will show clearly. You can also use 2×3s or 2×4s, which require toenailing but are more stable.

The easiest construction method is to build an L-shaped ladder frame on the floor, then secure it overhead by nailing or screwing one rail into the ceiling joists and the other into the wall studs.

RECESSED MEDICINE CABINETS: Most medicine cabinets are designed to fit within a standard stud space 14½ inches wide. If the cabinet is wider than that, or if its location does not align with the studs, you will have to frame an opening for it. If you are cutting only one stud, you should be able to use a single 2×4 for the header and the sill. Cut and fit vertical 2×4s for the sides of the opening, spacing them so the cabinet will just fit between them.

BLOCKING: Install special blocking within the wall frame to support bathroom accessories. Nail 2×6 or larger blocks between the studs where towel bars, grab bars, and other accessories will be installed. Typical heights above the floor are 72–84 inches for the top of a wall cabinet, 36–48 inches for a towel bar, and waist height for grab bars. Nail 2×4 blocks between the studs just above the rim of the bathtub to which the wall backing can be attached.

WINDOWS: When framing a window over a countertop, first determine the height of the finished sill. Will you place it flush with the countertop or above the back splash? If the finished windowsill will be flush with the countertop, be sure to take into account the thickness of the finish floor and of the countertop (if these have not yet been installed), as well as the thickness of the finished sill. Allow extra clearance for shimming when you lay out the height of the rough sill.

SKYLIGHTS: A bathroom skylight is framed just like any skylight. However, you will have less maneuvering room when you lay it out because the ceiling area is small and because the fixtures and any built-in cabinets will create strong axis lines. Normally, you have some leeway in locating a skylight so it can be positioned between rafters; but in a bathroom, you may have to cut through more rafters or ceiling joists than you anticipated just so you can align the skylight with other features of the room.

POCKET DOORS: Pocket doors are available in kits, including a frame that is recessed into the wall. When planning the header, allow for the frame, as well as for the door opening. There should be no plumbing, wiring, or other obstructions inside the wall where the frame goes.

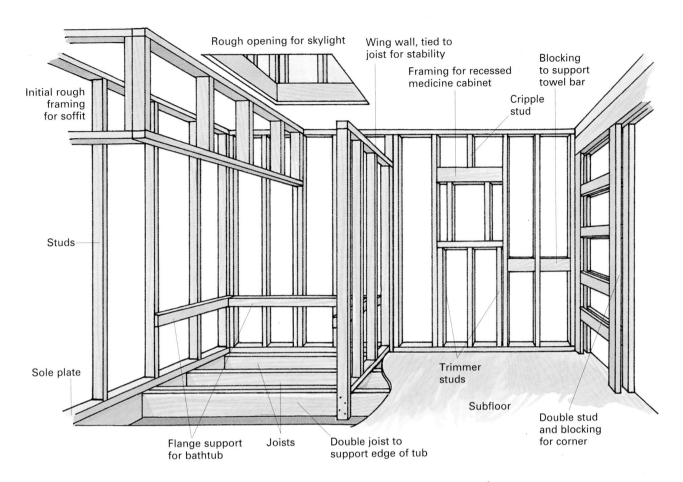

Rough opening for skylight

Wing wall, tied to joist for stability

Framing for recessed medicine cabinet

Blocking to support towel bar

Initial rough framing for soffit

Cripple stud

Studs

Sole plate

Trimmer studs

Subfloor

Double stud and blocking for corner

Flange support for bathtub

Joists

Double joist to support edge of tub

BATHTUBS: A bathtub built into an alcove or a corner is installed against the framing, not against the finished wall. The framed opening should be just large enough for the tub to slide into place against the studs. Adjust the stud spacing where the faucet will be installed so that a stud will not get in the way of the plumbing.

SHOWER STALLS: If you are using a prefabricated shower pan or stall, frame the walls so that it will fit snugly against the studs. (*See page 24 for more information.*)

PLUMBING

The bathroom is the most significant part of a residential plumbing system, so changing the plumbing can be complicated. Basic fixtures for most bathrooms are a toilet, a bathtub, a shower, and a lavatory, but your bathroom may also have a second sink, a bidet, or a steam room. Even if you don't plan to move fixtures, review this section to make sure the plumbing is adequate. Drainpipes and vent pipes should be considered first.

DRAINPIPES AND VENT PIPES: The main concerns for drainpipes and vent pipes are size, slope, and venting requirements;

rough-in dimensions; and use of proper fittings. A bathroom requires a branch drain, at least 3 inches in diameter, connected to the main drain of the house. Your present branch drain probably meets these specifications. Drainpipe sizes are determined by the number of fixtures. Typical required sizes are: toilet, 3 inches, inside diameter; shower, 2 inches; bathtub (with or without a shower), 1½ inches; bidet, 1½ inches; and lavatory, 1¼ inches. In practice, 1½-inch drainpipes are commonly used for sinks. If two sinks share the same drainpipe, it should have a 2-inch inside diameter, although a 1½-inch pipe may be allowed for the first vertical section. Check your local code.

If you are extending a drain, you must consider the slope. Drainpipes must slope ¼ inch per foot. So if the existing drain is strapped close to the bottom of the floor joists, there may not be enough clearance to extend it upstream to a new fixture. If the new pipe runs parallel to the joists, it can be suspended between them. Otherwise, it may be possible to bore through the joists for a 1½- or 2-inch drainpipe, provided the joists are 2×10s or 2×12s and the holes are at least 2 inches from the edge. Otherwise, it will be necessary to hang the new drainpipe below the joists and connect it to the main drain

MAKING STRUCTURAL IMPROVEMENTS
continued

farther downstream in order to get the proper flow. It is not necessary to vent all fixtures into the same branch drain. It may be more convenient to connect a new fixture to a different drain, as long as it is large enough.

All plumbing fixtures must be vented above the roof. If you are not moving a fixture far, you can probably use the original vent. A drainpipe must be vented within a certain distance (called the maximum trap arm distance) of the fixture trap and before it changes from horizontal to vertical. An exception is often made for the toilet drainpipe, which can be vented after it changes to vertical. Codes prohibit changing direction of the vent pipe from vertical to horizontal at any point lower than 6 inches above the flood rim of the fixture. This is typically a minimum of 36 inches above the floor for a lavatory, 21 inches for a toilet, and 20–26 inches for a bathtub.

If a window or other obstruction makes it necessary to change the direction of the vent pipe before this point, you have two choices:

The drain-waste-vent system relies on gravity and convection to carry away wastes and gas.

■ Offset the vent pipe with two 45-degree fittings to clear the obstruction.
■ Run the vertical vent pipe along one side of the window and run a horizontal trap arm from the fixture to the pipe (as long as it does not exceed the maximum trap arm distance). If you are venting a lavatory in an island, where a vertical vent pipe cannot be concealed in a wall, you can use a special loop arrangement. Check local code for venting requirements, such as maximum trap arm distance (typically 3 feet for a 1½-inch drainpipe and up to 5 feet for a 2-inch pipe).

Obtain rough-in dimensions from the supplier or manufacturer of each new fixture you plan to install. If you're replacing an old toilet, check the location of the floor flange. The rough-in dimension for most new toilets is 12 inches from the center of the flange to the surface of the finished wall behind it. Many older toilets were centered 10 or 14 inches from the wall. If this was the case with your old toilet, the new toilet may not fit, or it may be too far from the wall. If you are installing a wall-mounted toilet, you must install a separate carrier in the wall as part of the rough plumbing.

When roughing in drainpipes, maintain the proper slope and use the proper fitting for each connection and each change in direction. For instance, the tee fitting for a lavatory must be a fixture tee, not a sanitary tee, which looks almost identical. For double basins you can run the trap arms into a double fixture tee, which has a 2-inch outlet on the bottom, a 1½-inch outlet at the top, and a 1½-inch inlet on each side for the trap arms. If you are unsure about the proper fittings to use, consult a plumber.

Install the bathtub as part of the rough plumbing so you can fill it with water and test it before closing in any pipes. It is easiest to attach the trip-lever drain and overflow assembly first. Then slide the tub into position, being careful

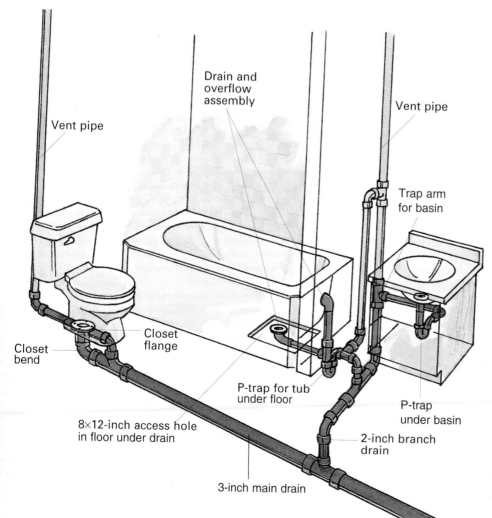

Vent pipe

Drain and overflow assembly

Vent pipe

Trap arm for basin

Closet flange

Closet bend

P-trap for tub under floor

P-trap under basin

8×12-inch access hole in floor under drain

2-inch branch drain

3-inch main drain

not to mar the surface. Avoid wearing watches, rings, and belt buckles that may rub against the tub while you're jostling it into place. A cast-iron tub will stay in place, but steel or fiberglass tubs must be supported at the rim with ledger boards; flanges must be secured against the framing with galvanized nails or screws.

If you're moving the toilet, you'll need to rough in a new floor flange. The top of the flange should be flush with the surface of the finish floor. If you will be adding underlayment to the floor after the flange is in place, you need to raise the flange to match. Cut an 8-inch-square piece of the underlayment or of some similar material, with a hole for the flange outlet, to put under the flange before installing it.

WATER SUPPLY PIPES: Run water pipes after drain and vent pipes are installed. The most popular supply-pipe choices are copper and PVC plastic, although some local codes prohibit using plastic. Galvanized pipes (which must be cut and threaded) are another alternative. Polybutylene (PB, a flexible plastic pipe) is allowed in some areas. The size of the pipes is determined by the number of fixtures being served, the water pressure, and the length of the runs. As a rule of thumb, use ½-inch pipe for all hot-water lines and for cold-water lines serving one fixture. Use ¾-inch pipe for cold-water lines serving more than one fixture.

If you connect copper to old galvanized pipes, use a dielectric union or intermediate brass fitting. This will help to prevent corrosion caused by joining dissimilar metals. If possible, it is better to replace old galvanized pipes now than to risk flooding your remodeled bathroom someday.

Typical rough-in dimensions for water supply stubs are 19 inches above the floor for a sink, 8 inches for a toilet, 26 inches for a bathtub, and 46 inches for a shower. You can adjust these dimensions to fit a manufacturer's specifications or your own needs. Double sinks should have separate stub-outs and shutoff valves.

You may want to add a second water heater to serve the new bathroom. It will increase the capacity of the system, and shorter runs will give you hot water faster. An electric heater can be located almost anywhere; some are small enough to fit inside a vanity. A gas heater must have a flue and a source of fresh air; certain bathroom, bedroom, and closet installations are prohibited. Check with the local building department to learn requirements in your area.

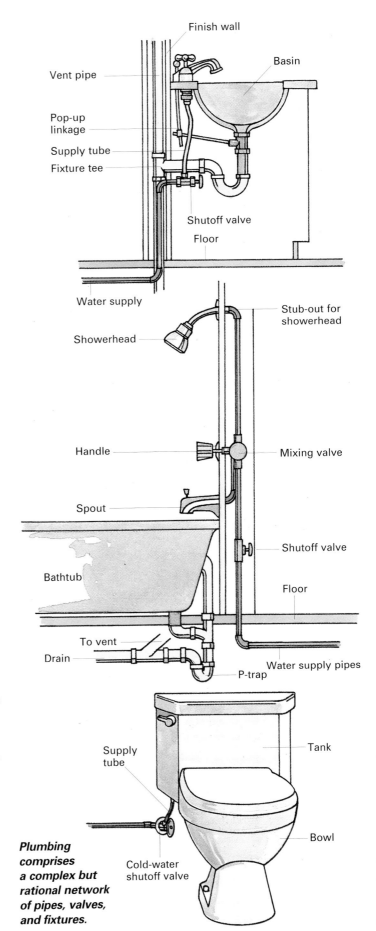

Plumbing comprises a complex but rational network of pipes, valves, and fixtures.

MAKING STRUCTURAL IMPROVEMENTS
continued

ROUGH WIRING

Wiring for most bathrooms involves:
■ Installing outlets for new light fixtures
■ Adding or moving switches
■ Adding or moving receptacles
■ Protecting receptacles with ground fault circuit interrupters (GFCIs), and
■ Adding new circuits for specific fixtures.

Techniques and code requirements are similar to those for other rooms, except the presence of water and grounded pipes makes safety an even more important issue. Abide by local code, which is likely to require:

■ A separate circuit should serve each permanently installed fixture above a certain amperage, such as a whirlpool bathtub, an electric wall heater, or an electric water heater. Radiant-heat lamps and ceiling fans may also require separate circuits.

■ All outlets and any motors for bathtub equipment must be protected by a GFCI device that automatically deadens the outlet the moment any unusual condition creates the potential for electric shock. These devices are available as circuit breakers installed in the main breaker panel (thus protecting an entire circuit) or as receptacles.

A GFCI receptacle can be wired so it protects other receptacles, as well. To prevent excessive nuisance tripping, it's best to install one that protects all the receptacles in the bathroom. That way the device is accessible and can be easily reset. Bathroom outlets do not usually require a separate circuit of their own. However, it may be necessary to run a new circuit if the existing house circuits are not grounded or if they are loaded to capacity.

■ Bathroom lights should be on a separate lighting circuit. They should not be tied to receptacles or individual fixtures.

■ For safety, no fixtures, switches, or outlets can be located within a certain distance of a tub (usually 5 feet horizontally and 7½ feet vertically, but check local code). You may be able to install lights or switches within that area if you protect them with GFCI devices, air switches, or low-voltage switch relays.

NEW CIRCUITS

As you plan new circuits, determine whether the present electrical system can meet the new demand. There are two things to consider: One is the available space for new circuit breakers, including a double space for each 240-volt breaker. The other is the electrical capacity of the main service entrance. If the present panel has few or no empty spaces for new breakers, you can use either half-size wafer breakers to get more space or install a subpanel (typically 60 amperes) for any new circuits. Check with the local building department to determine where the subpanel may be installed. Closets or other restricted spaces may not be allowed.

Most houses have enough electrical capacity to meet the added demands of a new bathroom, provided you are not adding any major appliances, such as a water heater. The present service must be properly grounded, however, and it must be at least 100 amperes. If in any doubt, have a load calculation done by an electrical contractor to be sure that the demand won't overload the system. If it will, you will have to upgrade the service entrance.

ELECTRICAL BOXES: Locate boxes for lights, switches, and outlets according to the design plan. Avoid locating boxes for receptacles where they might interfere with a mirror, a medicine cabinet, a towel bar, or a complicated back splash. If the box must be installed in the side of a vanity, you must use flexible armored cable where the wiring is exposed inside the cabinet.

Note: Most boxes extend ½ inch out from the studs to accommodate the thickness of standard wallboard. However, some outlets may be located within the back splash area. Be sure to extend the box far enough out to accommodate both the wallboard and the back splash material. The face of the box must be flush with the finished surface.

ELECTRICAL CABLE: For most installations, the codes will allow the use of Romex nonmetallic sheathed cable. Use No. 12 for 20-ampere circuits and No. 10 or larger for 240-volt circuits. Observe the same rules for running cable in a bathroom as in any other room. Staple it every 4½ feet and within 8 inches of plastic boxes or within 12 inches of metal boxes. Many building codes do not allow wiring to be run horizontally through exterior wall studs; it must be run under the floor and brought up through the sole-plate for each outlet. Check your local code.

CONSTRUCTION TIP

When working with new wiring, always check the local code to be sure you're doing the work properly.

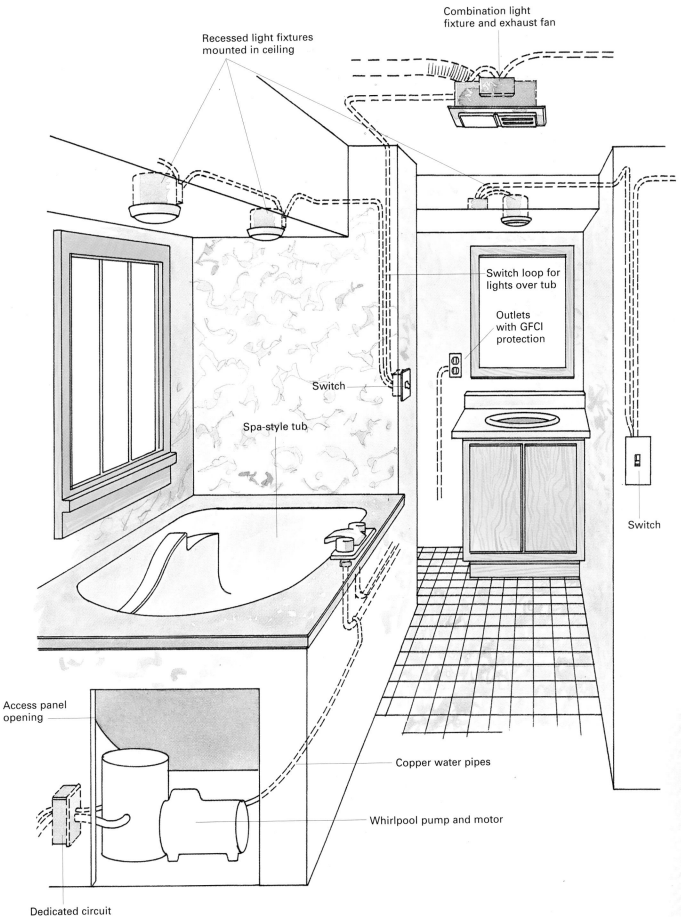

Recessed light fixtures
mounted in ceiling

Combination light
fixture and exhaust fan

Switch loop for
lights over tub

Outlets
with GFCI
protection

Switch

Spa-style tub

Switch

Access panel
opening

Copper water pipes

Whirlpool pump and motor

Dedicated circuit
for whirlpool motor

HEATING AND VENTILATION

There are several ways to add a heating system to the bathroom. You can extend an existing forced-air system, extend an existing hot-water (hydronic) system, or install a new electric baseboard or wall heater.

Because wall space in bathrooms is limited, you may have difficulty finding a good location for a forced-air register. The usual solution is to locate it under the front edge of the vanity cabinet by bringing a duct up through the floor or out from the back wall. Run a transition elbow or a straight rectangular duct on the floor where the vanity will go; cut a hole in the front of the toe kick; and set the vanity in place. Cover the hole with a 3¼×10-inch adjustable-louvered grill.

Electric wall heaters are wired with either a 120-volt or a 240-volt circuit. The 240-volt circuit requires three-wire cable and a double circuit breaker. Cost is offset by the more efficient use of electricity.

An exhaust fan is desirable in any bathroom and is generally required in bathrooms without operable windows. All fans should be ducted directly outside through the roof or a nearby wall. To install a fan, set the housing in place between two ceiling joists. Install a termination cap in the wall or roof by cutting a hole approximately 4½ inches in diameter through the sheathing and attaching the cap from the outside. Run 4-inch flexible duct from the fan housing to the termination cap. Secure it at each end, using a tightening band or sheet-metal screws.

Run a two-wire No. 12 feeder cable from the circuit breaker panel to the fan junction box, then run cable from the fan to a switch box on the wall. Use one 2-wire, one 3-wire, or two 2-wire cables (all with ground wires), depending on how many switches are needed to control the appliance you're wiring for. All of the wires in this switch loop will be hot, so mark any white wires with black tape.

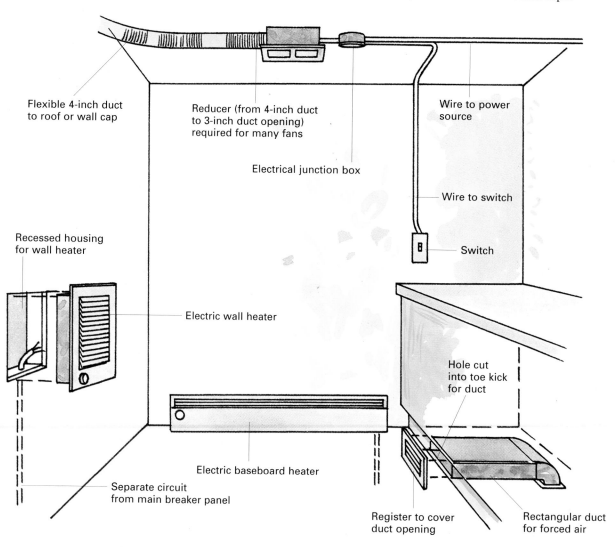

Flexible 4-inch duct to roof or wall cap

Reducer (from 4-inch duct to 3-inch duct opening) required for many fans

Electrical junction box

Wire to power source

Wire to switch

Switch

Recessed housing for wall heater

Electric wall heater

Hole cut into toe kick for duct

Electric baseboard heater

Separate circuit from main breaker panel

Register to cover duct opening

Rectangular duct for forced air

PREPARING WALLS AND CEILINGS

Walls and ceiling of a bathroom are covered in the usual way. They are also insulated in the usual way. However, it is advisable to staple polyethylene sheeting over the insulation before applying wallboard to protect it against damage from water vapor. Use a utility knife to cut out the sheeting around obstructions, such as windows and electrical boxes.

Wallboard is also installed in the standard manner, although you may have to make numerous cutouts for plumbing, wiring, and mechanical devices. Special moisture resistant wallboard is available for areas likely to get wet. Use it around the lavatory, in the upper wall of a shower stall or bathtub enclosure, or in areas where tile will be installed over a mortar bed. Use mesh tape and waterproof joint compound to cover the joints. Moisture resistant wallboard is heavy, so it must be well-fastened if it is used on the ceiling. Do not use it as a tub or shower backing in areas where the tile will not be set in a mortar bed—special nonorganic tile-backing units work better. If you are patching new wallboard into old wallboard or plaster, cut the old material back to a corner, a door, a window, or some other feature in order to make the joint less obvious.

There are several methods for patching holes in old wallboard. Small holes can be filled with patching compound; you may want to cover them first with adhesive-backed fiberglass mesh tape. Trim larger holes to a regular shape, such as a triangle. Cut a patch of wallboard to fit exactly into the hole and a wide strip of plywood or wallboard to serve as backing. Slip the backing strip inside the wall behind the hole and secure it with wallboard screws or paneling adhesive. Glue or screw the patch to the backing and tape the seams. Large holes can be patched by cutting the wallboard back to the nearest studs and fitting in a new piece. Baseboard and other trim can be installed at this point, except where it abuts built-in fixtures.

Any surfaces that will be painted, whether old or new, must be clean, dry, and free of peeling paint. Use abrasive paper or trisodium phosphate (TSP) to roughen glossy surfaces so new paint will stick. Final painting can be done before or after fixtures and cabinets are installed (it's easier to do beforehand). Do the ceiling first, to avoid spattering paint on new fixtures and cabinets.

Wallpaper and similar coverings are usually applied last, but you may want to apply them before installing the fixtures and cabinets if you can be sure they won't be soiled or damaged during the final stages of construction. Prepare the wall surfaces as you would for painting. Some wallpapers may adhere to an unsized wall so follow the dealer's recommendations regarding sizing. (See page 89 for information on finishing walls.)

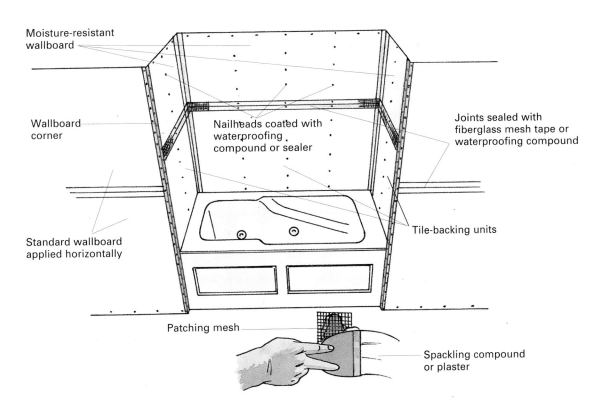

Moisture-resistant wallboard

Wallboard corner

Standard wallboard applied horizontally

Nailheads coated with waterproofing compound or sealer

Joints sealed with fiberglass mesh tape or waterproofing compound

Tile-backing units

Patching mesh

Spackling compound or plaster

INSTALLING FIXTURES

When it comes to installing fixtures, preparation is often nine-tenths of the job. The following guidelines explain how to install each bathroom fixture from start to finish.

Usually, you will not do all the work on a given fixture at once. Rather, you'll do some part of the work for all of the fixtures at the same time. For example, you'll do all the framing at once, all the rough plumbing, installing wallboard and tile, and then all the finish plumbing.

Dual spray heads offer a luxurious all-over shower. Niches in this tiled shower stall serve as shelves for everything from soap to shower gel. The lower shelf is placed at a comfortable height for children to use.

SHOWER STALLS

You have three options for a new shower stall. You can choose a prefabricated, one-piece unit; a custom-built stall with a prefabricated shower pan; or a custom-built stall with a custom-built shower pan. A prefabricated unit is the easiest to install. If you have basic carpentry, plumbing, and ceramic tile-setting skills, you can build a shower stall with a prefabricated base.

PREFABRICATED UNITS: Plastic or fiberglass prefab units, which include everything except the plumbing, can be installed by one person in less than a day. The most difficult part may be getting the unit into the bathroom since it may not pass through a standard doorway. Some units have a ceiling; others don't.

■ Build conventional framed walls to support the unit. Space studs evenly and adjust spacing where the plumbing will be installed so that the studs will not interfere with the faucet. The width of the enclosure must be exact, so check the manufacturer's specifications or measure the unit at its base.
NOTE: Some local codes may require you to install fireproof wallboard in the opening before installing the shower. This provision often applies particularly to buildings with multiple dwelling units.

■ Rough in a 2-inch P-trap under the floor and install the 2-inch drainpipe where the drain hole will go. Cut it off at the height specified by the manufacturer's instructions. Rough in the faucet and showerhead and cut holes in the walls of the stall to fit the showerhead pipe and faucet stems.

■ Install the drain fitting in the floor of the shower, using plumber's putty around the flange. Remove the gasket and retaining ring.

■ Lift the shower unit into place, centering the drain fitting down over the drain pipe. Some manufacturers recommend setting the unit on a ½-inch bed of mortar or quick-setting plaster compound to provide maximum support. Nail the top and side flanges to the studs with galvanized roofing nails. Secure the drain fitting by slipping the gasket down around the 2-inch drainpipe and screwing the retaining ring down on it to compress it.

■ Finish plumbing the faucet and the showerhead. Apply caulk around cutouts and attach the fittings and escutcheons to the rough plumbing. Test the plumbing.

■ Apply wallboard or other wallcovering to the framing, bringing it over the wall flanges of the shower unit. Finish the wallcovering to match the surrounding areas—with paint, wallpaper, tile, or other materials.

BUILDING A SHOWER STALL

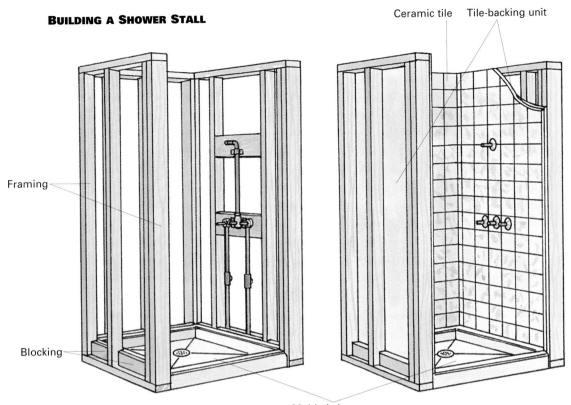

Ceramic tile   Tile-backing unit

Framing

Blocking

Molded shower pan

CUSTOM-BUILT STALLS: You will need to have the dimensions of the shower pan or the pan itself on hand before framing the walls. Before beginning construction, decide what special features you want. For instance, shower faucet handles are normally set 42–48 inches above the floor; showerheads are typically 66–78 inches above the floor. However, you may want to put the handles at a different height, or set several showerheads, activated individually, at different heights to accommodate different users. You can also plan to have grab bars, a seat, or recessed shelves or alcoves.

■ Construct the side that will take the plumbing. Set it at a right angle to the back wall. Space the studs so they will not interfere with the plumbing and nail blocking between the studs where the top edge of the shower pan will go.

■ Rough in a 2-inch P-trap under the floor, with a vertical drain stub coming up through the floor where the drain hole will go. Rough in the water supply pipes, the shower valve, and the elbow for the showerhead. If possible, provide shutoff valves that can be reached from an access door on the back of the plumbing wall.

■ Install the shower pan according to the instructions provided by the manufacturer.

■ Finish framing around the pan. At the top of the pan, insert blocking between the studs. Secure the nailing flanges to the studs and blocking with galvanized roofing nails.

■ Apply 15-pound roofing paper over the frame for the shower stall. Start at the bottom and overlap sheets as you work upward.

■ Cover the roofing paper with tile-backing units up to the point where the tile will end. Most brands of backing come in 3×5-foot panels, but some manufacturers also offer 4×5-foot and 4×8-foot panels. Nail them to the studs with galvanized roofing nails, lapping the backing over the flange of the shower pan. Leave a ¼-inch gap around the bottom of the panels. Seal the joints with fiberglass mesh tape and waterproof joint compound or tile adhesive. Cover the upper portion of the stall and the outside of the walls with wallboard.

■ Finish the inside of the stall with tile, marble, or other appropriate material. Finish the outside to match the surrounding walls. Install the finish plumbing and a glass shower door according to manufacturer's instructions (*see page 95*). If you have to drill holes into the tile to secure the doorframe, use a carbide-tipped bit. If possible, align the holes with the grout lines to make drilling easier.

INSTALLING FIXTURES
continued

BATHTUBS

Install bathtubs as part of the rough plumbing before the walls are closed in and the floor is finished. The tub is the hardest of all bathroom fixtures to install, for the same reasons that it is the hardest to remove. It is big, cumbersome, heavy, and the plumbing connections are usually made inside a tight space. To install even a lightweight fiberglass tub, you will need at least one helper; if the bathtub is made of cast iron, you will want several.

For purposes of installation, there are two types of bathtub. Tubs with one finished side are designed to be installed in an alcove. Tubs with no finished sides are designed to be surrounded by a built-in platform. Differences in size, material, and configuration can pose special problems, however, so be sure to get installation instructions from the dealer or manufacturer.

This elegant, oversized bathtub invites old-fashioned soaks. Unglazed ceramic tiles on floors and walls create a neutral backdrop.

BUILT-IN TUBS: The following guidelines explain how to install a standard 30×60-inch enameled steel tub. They should give you a general sense of how to install any bathtub in an alcove.

■ Frame walls so the opening is just large enough to slide the tub into place against the studs. End studs should be recessed slightly so the surface of the wallcovering will be flush with the finished side of the tub. Adjust stud spacings so the studs will not interfere with installation of the faucet.

■ Slide the tub into place, level it with shims under the bottom, and mark where the bottom of the rim touches the studs. Pull the tub out again and nail 2×4 ledgers to the studs just under the marks. These ledgers will support the rim of the tub. Mark, measure, and nail carefully. The ledger boards must be the right height off the floor to enable the rim to make full contact. Slide the tub in again and double-check your measurements. If the P-trap has not yet been roughed in, mark on the floor the center of the drain hole. Slide the tub back out.

■ If the P-trap and drainpipe have not been roughed in, cut an access hole in the floor approximately 4–6 inches wide extending 12 inches from the center of the end wall. Rough in a 1½-inch P-trap below floor level, with the slip-nut fitting centered directly under the overflow pipe of the tub.

■ You can rough in the water supply pipes, the mixing valve, and the stubs for the spout and showerhead now or after the tub is installed, depending on how easy it will be to get behind the tub later. The spout is usually installed 4 inches above the tub rim, the faucets 4–6 inches above the spout, and the showerhead 66–78 inches above the floor. You can adjust these heights to suit your needs. Install shutoff valves for the hot and cold water lines.

■ Connect the drain elbow to the tub, applying a ring of plumber's putty under the flange. Hold the drain-tee steady with the handle of a pair of pliers while you tighten the nut underneath. You can attach the overflow pipe and the tailpiece now or when the tub is in place. Cut the tailpiece so it will fit 1–1½ inches down into the P-trap.

■ If the tub is not insulated, fit fiberglass blanket insulation around it. If there is room, put some under the tub. Do not compress the insulation.

■ Slide the tub into place and use shims where necessary to make it stable and level. Drive 7d or 8d galvanized box nails above the steel flange and into the studs so the nails hold the flange to the walls. If the tub is made of fiberglass, drill pilot holes into the flange before you nail through it. A cast-iron tub need not be secured to the walls.

■ Connect the drain. The tailpiece below the drain tee should slide into the P-trap below the floor. Tighten the slip joints on the P-trap and the drain tee securely. Install the stopper mechanism according to the manufacturer's instructions.

To test for leaks and prepare for the plumbing inspection, fill the tub with water and let it sit for a few hours. Open the stopper and let the water run down the drain.

■ Apply tile-backing units or moisture resistant wallboard (depending on the finish material) to the framing around the tub. Lap it over the tub flange but leave a ¼-inch gap around the top of the rim. This gap should be caulked when the tile or other finish material is installed. Seal the joints with fiberglass mesh tape and moisture-resistant joint compound or tile adhesive.

■ If you install tile, use a level to mark guidelines for the first (bottom) row of tiles. Not all tub rims are level, so don't use the tub rim as a guide.

PLATFORM TUBS: Most luxury tubs, whether they are whirlpool units or conventional models, are designed for platform installation. Some come with an optional matching skirt to finish the side, but most units are finished with custom materials applied over a frame that is built on-site.

The guidelines presented here are applicable to most installations, but you may need to modify them to accommodate a specific type of tub, choice of finish, or plumbing detail. For example, if the tub is light enough to allow two or three people to lift it into place, you can build the platform first and then lower the tub into it.

You may have to exercise ingenuity in doing some finish work before you do the plumbing so that the rim of the tub will rest on a finished surface. If you want the rim to be covered or to be flush with the surrounding surface, finish the platform deck at the same time as you finish the sides.

In some cases, there may not be room to install a platform all the way around the tub, so the finished walls will come down to the rim as they do on a built-in tub.

Tubs made of acrylic and other plastic materials can expand and contract with changes in temperature; they must have strong support around the rim.

■ It is usually easier to install the tub first and then build the supporting framework so it fits properly. This is the only option if the tub is made of cast iron. Be sure the drain line and P-trap are roughed in below the floor and there is an access hole through the floor for connecting the tub drain to the P-trap.

■ Build the frame out of 2×4s, spacing the studs 14½ inches apart (16 inches "on center," the distance from the center of one stud to the center of the next). Attach the framing to the walls and floor with screws or with nails and construction glue. If you want a wider ledge, use 2×6 lumber or build another 2×4 frame outside the first one. Build a third frame if you want the platform to be more than 16 inches wide. You can rough in the water supply pipes now.

■ Using pry bars, raise the tub about 1 inch and support it temporarily on blocks. Apply moisture resistant backing to the top of the framing and seal the joints with mesh tape. Install tile or other finish material along the top of the ledge where it will be covered by the rim of the tub. Plan the layout carefully to allow for an overhang around the outside edge. If you plan to install a deck-mounted faucet or spout, remember to allow for the holes. After the adhesives have set up thoroughly, spread a ½-inch layer of mortar or quick-setting plaster on the floor and lower the tub onto it. For a watertight seal, apply a

INSTALLING FIXTURES
continued

bead of caulk around the bottom of the rim before you lower the tub.

■ Hook up the drain as you would for a built-in tub. Some drains are located along the side of the tub and others at one end.

■ Rough in the water supply pipes and install the mixing valve and spout. If there is an integral filler spout below the rim of the tub, you will need to install a vacuum breaker between this spout and the mixing valve. Because the vacuum breaker must be mounted at least 6 inches above the rim of the tub, you will have to run the water line from the mixing valve back to the nearest wall, up the wall to the vacuum breaker, and back to the spout. The breaker must be accessible for servicing, so install a removable panel or door on one side of the wall.

■ If the tub has a whirlpool unit, it will probably come with the motor and circulating pipes installed. Feed wires for the motor should be connected to a separate circuit.

Most local codes require that all metal pipes be bonded to the motor with a separate No. 6 copper ground wire. Some codes also require that the ground wire between the motor and the house grounding system be continuous, and that it be separate from the electrical conduit or cable. The switch activating the motor must have an approved safety protection device, such as a GFCI.

■ Test the plumbing for leaks by filling the tub. Do not test a whirlpool until there is enough water in the tub to cover all the jets.

■ After the plumbing has been inspected, insulate the tub (*see page 78*) and cover the framing with a backing appropriate to the finish material. The latter may be tile, dimensioned-stone, solid-surface material, or wood. If the tub has a whirlpool, install a removable panel for access to the motor.

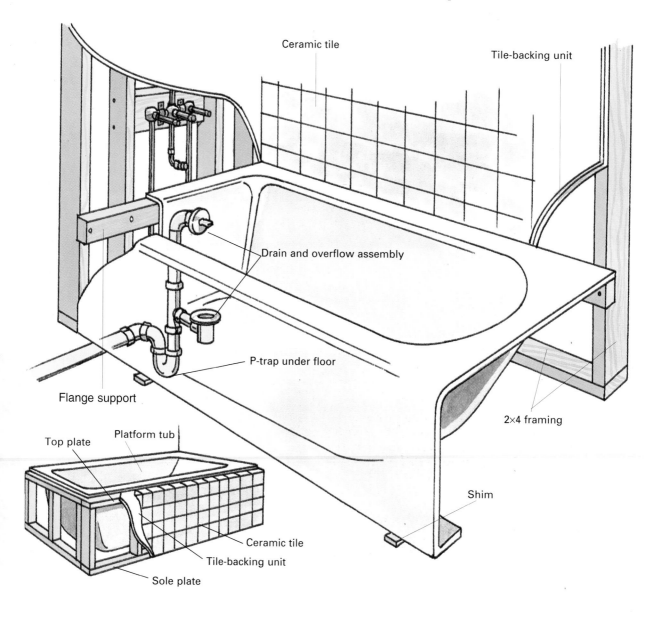

Ceramic tile

Tile-backing unit

Drain and overflow assembly

P-trap under floor

Flange support

2×4 framing

Shim

Top plate

Platform tub

Ceramic tile

Tile-backing unit

Sole plate

VANITY CABINETS

It is relatively easy to install a vanity. It's also easy to individualize one to meet your special needs. If you want a large vanity, you can combine two or more modular units, or you can have a cabinet custom-made. Standard height for vanity countertops is 30–32 inches, but you can make yours higher.

■ Vanity cabinets are generally open in back to accommodate plumbing. If yours is not, cut out a section of the back for the water supply and drain stubs. You can install the shutoff valves after the vanity is in place, but it's easier to install them beforehand.

■ Be sure the floor is level. If it's not, put shims under the cabinet or trim down the base to level it. Walls surrounding the cabinet should be flat without any bumps or bulges.

■ If you wish to make the vanity or countertop higher, there are several ways to do it. Use a modular kitchen base cabinet, which is 34½ inches high and 24 inches deep. Or build a base out of 2×4s and set the vanity on top of it. You can raise the toe kick by turning the cabinet over and screwing wood cleats to the bottom. Or elevate the countertop by screwing cleats to the top of the vanity and attaching the countertop to them. Finish the cleats to match the vanity.

■ To install your vanity, first measure the height of the cabinet. Using a level, draw a line on the wall at that height. If the vanity is in a corner, draw lines on both walls. Drill pilot holes into the hanging cleat on the cabinet. Center each hole over a wall stud. Attach the hanging cleat to the wall with 2½-inch screws. Be sure the weight of the cabinet rests on the floor, not on the screws.

■ If you combine two or more units, fasten them together with C-clamps. Drill pilot holes into the side of the stile of one cabinet and drive screws through these holes into the stile of the adjacent unit. Make sure cabinets are level and face frames are tight and flush. Tightening the screws often pulls a unit out of line. If this happens, adjust it with shims.

Recycling a charming antique adds an elegant touch of old-fashioned warmth in this otherwise plain bathroom. Let antiques dealers know you're looking for a piece with a flawed top—you're going to cut a hole in it anyway—and you may find a bargain. Be sure the piece is finished with a preservative or paint to protect it from the bath's moist environment.

INSTALLING FIXTURES
continued

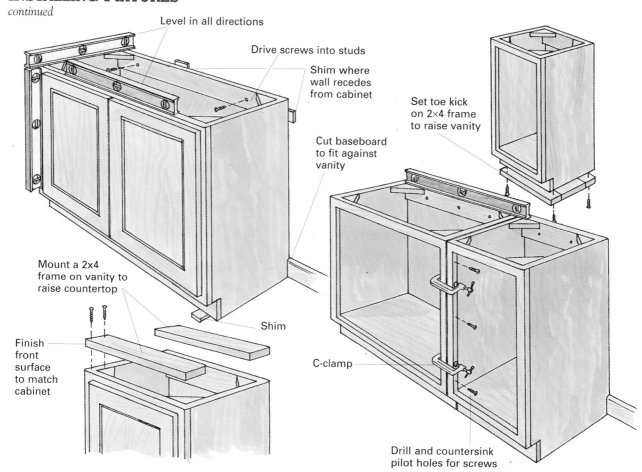

Level in all directions

Drive screws into studs

Shim where wall recedes from cabinet

Set toe kick on 2×4 frame to raise vanity

Cut baseboard to fit against vanity

Mount a 2x4 frame on vanity to raise countertop

Finish front surface to match cabinet

Shim

C-clamp

Drill and countersink pilot holes for screws

COUNTERTOPS

Each type of countertop has a distinct installation technique, but all are similar in certain respects. In taking measurements, allow for a 1-inch overhang in front of the vanity. Allow for a ½-inch overhang on any side that does not abut a wall. There should be a back splash and, if necessary, side splashes to prevent water from marring the walls and seeping down behind the cabinet. The back splash is usually 4 inches high.

The easiest countertop to install is one made of cast polymer or solid surface material with a lavatory molded into it. All you have to do is run a bead of silicone caulk around the top edge of the cabinet and set the countertop into place. It's usually easiest to install the faucet and drain fitting beforehand. To install any other type of countertop, you must cut out a hole for the sink and add a back splash. With some materials you can build and install the countertop yourself; with others you can do the installation, but you should hire a professional to measure and fabricate the countertop.

CERAMIC TILE: Installing a tile countertop is a simple do-it-yourself project using the technique described here. Plan trim and accent pieces early and order them along with the tile. If the tile will be trimmed with a wood edge, the wood should be installed, stained, and sealed before you set the tile.

■ Prepare the substrate. An acceptable installation for a bathroom counter is ½-inch tile-backing units screwed and glued to a ¾-inch plywood base. Tile can also be laid directly over plywood, but the plywood must be sealed with an epoxy-based mastic; latex or epoxy modifiers must be added to the grout mix; and the grout must be sealed after it sets.

Start by installing a ¾-inch plywood base over the vanity. If you are not adding a mortar float or tile-backing units to the top, raise the plywood by attaching 1×3 strips to the bottom along the edges. This provides a backing for the tiles along the front edge and keeps them from interfering with the drawers. Screw in the top from below to make future removal easier. Check to make sure it is level. If it is not, level it by inserting shims between the vanity and the plywood.

Cut out the basin hole (see page 86). If you are installing a recessed lavatory, set it in place now. Use the method described for slab countertops if the tile will be flush with the top of the basin rim. If you plan to surround the sink with quarter-round trim, clamp the sink to the bottom of the base with special mounting clips that screw into plywood. Surface-mounted sinks are installed after the tiling is done.

■ Lay out the tile pattern and test it with a dry run, placing all tiles exactly where you want them. Start with the trim pieces, edging tiles first, and continue with the field tiles. Use tile spacers for uniform grout lines. If possible, avoid narrow cuts in the back. Trim pieces should be laid out so the grout lines follow the grout lines of the field tiles.

■ When you're satisfied with the layout for the front and back edges, lay out the tiles around the sink. If the sink will be surface-mounted, mark the tiles for cutting by laying them in place and scribing them from underneath. Cut them with a tile cutter or nippers. The rim of the sink will cover the raw edges.

If the sink is recessed, fit the trim pieces around it. Cut the tiles where they abut the trim pieces, allowing for the grout line. Make these cuts smoothly and accurately because the raw edges will remain visible. It's best to make them as you set the tile.

■ When you have completed the layout, remove the tiles and mark any pieces to be cut. In a large bucket, using special mortar-mixing paddles, mix adhesives according to package directions. Thinset adhesives are a combination of liquid and dry materials. Mix only the amount you will be able to use in about 1 hour. Let the mixed adhesive rest about 10 minutes before applying.

Adhesive is first spread, then combed.

Use a notched trowel for both steps. Check the instructions on the package to find how long the opened adhesive will remain workable. Also note any safety precautions regarding ventilation, open flames, and skin contact.

Start at one of the front corners, installing bullnose tiles or trim pieces first. Use spacers to keep the tiles evenly aligned. Place each tile carefully and press it down with a slight twisting motion.

■ Spread adhesive over a small area, holding the notched trowel at about a 45-degree angle. When you have installed all of the trim pieces, install the field tiles. Continue across the surface of the countertop. Use nippers to cut tiles so they fit around obstructions. When you have set the last row of countertop tiles, work your way up the back splash. Finish the top edge with bullnose tiles.

When all tiles are set, remove the excess mastic as quickly as possible. Let the work dry for one or two days.

Colorful ceramic tile requires minimal maintenance and provides a moisture-proof countertop ideal for bathrooms.

INSTALLING FIXTURES
continued

■ Grout the joints, following manufacturer's instructions. Spread the grout with a rubber float, working it diagonally to the grout lines. Force the grout firmly into the joints, using the handle of a toothbrush or some other small tool. Clean off excess grout with a damp sponge, wringing it out frequently in clean water. Let the surface residue dry to form a haze, then polish the tiles with cheesecloth or other soft cloth. Cover the countertop with plastic sheeting for two or three days to let the grout cure properly. After two weeks, seal the grout to keep it clean and free of mildew.

PLASTIC LAMINATE: High-pressure laminate is only about $1/16$-inch thick, so it must be bonded to a stable substrate of particleboard or plywood. You can do this yourself, provided you're familiar with the process. Otherwise, buy a length of ready-made postformed countertop or order a custom-made unit from a specialty shop. Have the fabricator install the countertop, or install it yourself using the following techniques.

■ Determine how long the countertop should be. Remember to allow for overhangs and for the thickness of the back splash pieces on the ends. Buy the next longest size. Buy separate end splash pieces and end caps, as needed.

■ Cut the countertop to length. Use a framing square to mark the cutting line along the top of the counter and up the back splash. If the corner of the wall is out of square, adjust the cutting line to compensate.

Place masking tape over the line and make a fresh mark on the masking tape. This will protect the edge from chipping when it's cut. Support the countertop well on both sides of the cutting line to prevent it from breaking.

Use a sharp handsaw with 10–12 teeth per inch, a reciprocating saw, or a circular saw with a sharp blade. If using a handsaw, bear lightly on the upstrokes and heavily on the downstrokes. If using a reciprocating saw, the teeth should point downward. If they do not, transfer the cutting line to the bottom of the countertop and cut from that side. Do the same thing with a circular saw. Smooth the edge of the cut with a file or plane.

■ Attach the end pieces. Where an end splash is required, the piece is usually a simple rectangle with the laminate applied to one side, one long edge, and both short edges. Fit it so the top edge is flush with the top of the back splash and the front edge is flush with the front of the countertop. Attach it to the end of the countertop with screws and water-resistant glue. Drill pilot holes for the screws.

If the counter has no end splash, cover the exposed edge with a special end cap. To support this piece, glue or screw $1/2$-inch by $1/2$-inch wood strips to the bottom and back of the countertop, flush with the end. Sand them smooth and glue the end cap in place with contact cement, following instructions on the container.

■ Seal the bottom of the countertop with primer or wood sealer to prevent possible damage from moisture.

■ Set the countertop in place, snug against the back wall and the sidewalls. If there are gaps due to irregularities in the wall, scribe the top of the back splash with a pencil. Hold the pencil vertical and flat against the wall and run the point along the top of the back splash. Pull the countertop out from the wall and trim away any excess on the backside of the line with a file, a block plane, or a belt sander.

Lay out the cutting line for the sink hole. Many manufacturers provide a template you can trace. If you have no template, turn the sink upside down in position and trace around it. Remove the sink and draw the cutting line about $1/2$ inch inside the tracing. This $1/2$-inch allowance will support the rim of the sink and still clear the bowl. Leave about 2 inches of counter in front of and behind the rim.

■ Cut a piece of 1×2 or similar scrap lumber 2 inches longer than the cutout for the sink hole. Attach it to the countertop by driving a single screw through the center of the board and into the center of the cutout. This board will keep the cutout from dropping through the hole before you finish sawing, which might cause the laminate to chip or break.

Drill a $3/4$-inch hole inside the line. Insert the blade of a saber saw into this hole and start the cut. When you reach the back splash, you may not have enough room to maneuver the saw. In that case, cut from the bottom of the countertop or use a keyhole saw. Round the corners on the cutout (square corners tend to start cracks).

■ If you're adding a back splash to the countertop, attach it next. Drill pilot holes along the back edge of the countertop and lay down a thick bead of silicone sealant. Set the back splash in place and drive screws up through the pilot holes to secure it. Clean up excess sealant immediately.

■ Fasten the countertop to the vanity from below, using screws long enough to penetrate $1/2$ inch into the countertop. Use self-driving screws or drill pilot holes through the cleats of the cabinets before setting the top down on them. Last of all, apply a thin bead of caulk between the countertop and the wall.

SOLID SURFACE MATERIAL: Solid surface countertops come as prefinished slabs that can be installed using basic woodworking techniques. They include cast polymers or products known by brand names such as Corian, Fountainhead, Avonite, and 2000X.

■ If you are mounting the lavatory under the countertop, begin by installing a ¾-inch plywood base over the vanity.

Cut out the sink hole, then rout a groove around the edge of the hole so the rim of the sink rests flush with the top of the plywood. Install the sink and support it by attaching cleats under the edge of the opening.

■ Measure and cut the countertop and the back splash. Use a circular saw with a carbide-tipped blade and cut from the backside. Wear goggles to protect your eyes when cutting. Clamp a straightedge to the countertop to guide the saw. Protect the surface with tape.

■ To create a thicker edge, turn the top over and attach trim pieces along the edge of the bottom with an adhesive recommended by the manufacturer. Clamp the joints and let them dry overnight before sanding them. Attach the back splash in the same way or attach it after the top is in place.

■ Shape the edges with a router, if you wish. With carbide bits you can create soft rounds, ogees, coves, bevels, and more elaborate shapes. Smooth the cut surfaces with abrasive paper.

■ Mark the sink hole and cut it out. Cut straight lines with a circular saw and corners with a router or a reciprocating saw,

depending on the manufacturer's recommendations. Set the top in place and check for fit.

■ Attach the countertop to the plywood base or to the top of the cabinet with a sealing caulk or mastic recommended by the manufacturer. Press the top firmly into the sealant for about 10 minutes.

■ Attach the back splash if you did not do so earlier. Seal all joints with a caulk, such as neoprene or silicone, as recommended by the manufacturer. Wipe away the excess and smooth the sealant with a damp rag wrapped around your finger.

STONE COUNTERTOPS: Marble and other natural stone must be cut and installed with specialized tools, a job best left to professionals. Decide how you want the sink mounted before you purchase the materials, because this will make a difference in the size of the sink hole, which is often cut out by the supplier. Be sure to seal and maintain the marble to prevent stains.

CONSTRUCTION TIPS

If you're replacing an old sink with a new one, you may find the new sink does not align exactly with the old plumbing. You can usually accommodate the new fixture by hooking it up with flexible connectors. It is difficult to crawl around under a sink, especially when it's installed in a vanity. Make your task easier by attaching as many fittings as possible to the sink before setting it into place.

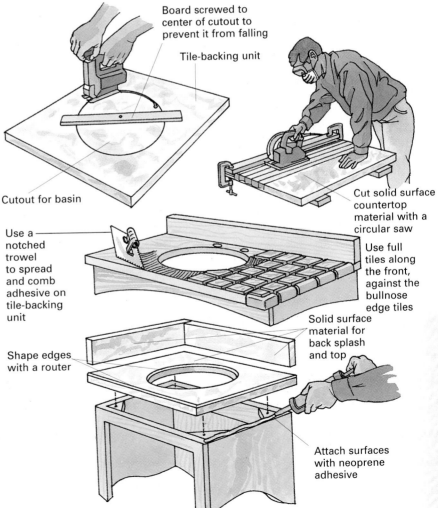

Board screwed to center of cutout to prevent it from falling

Tile-backing unit

Cutout for basin

Cut solid surface countertop material with a circular saw

Use a notched trowel to spread and comb adhesive on tile-backing unit

Shape edges with a router

Use full tiles along the front, against the bullnose edge tiles

Solid surface material for back splash and top

Attach surfaces with neoprene adhesive

INSTALLING FIXTURES
continued

SINKS

Wall-mounted, pedestal, and countertop sinks are all installed in much the same way, but they're installed at different points in the sequence of construction.

■ Sinks recessed below a countertop must be installed before the finish material is applied. This material will either cover the rim or butt up to it for a flush surface.

■ Sinks mounted on a countertop are installed after the finish material. Some have a self-rim; others have a separate metal rim that creates a low profile.

■ Pedestal sinks are installed after the walls are finished and floor coverings are in place. Before covering the walls, make sure studs or blocking are positioned to support the sink.

ATTACHING FITTINGS: To attach the drain fitting to the sink, unscrew the flange piece from the top of the drainpipe. Screw the tightening nut down to the bottom of the threads and slip the washer and gasket over the threads all the way down to the tightening nut. Apply plumber's putty around the top edge of the drain hole. Insert the drain fitting through the hole from below. Screw the flange down onto it, then tighten the nut under the sink to draw the flange piece snugly onto the putty. Attach the faucet according to the manufacturer's instructions.

■ A one-piece, center-set faucet is the easiest to install. It has two bolts or threaded stubs that are inserted down through the sink holes. Attach nuts from below, then connect the water supply lines to the threaded stubs.

■ Single-control units have two copper supply lines attached to the faucet. Connect these to the shutoff valves.

■ Wide-set faucets are more complicated. They have a spout and two handle units, all of which are inserted through holes in the basin or countertop. Working from underneath, connect each handle unit to the spout with flexible hosing or copper tubing provided by the manufacturer. Attach hot and cold supply lines to the handle units.

Install the linkage for the pop-up drain assembly. It may be easier to do this after the sink is in place.

COUNTERTOP SINKS: A recessed sink is installed in the plywood countertop before the finish material is applied. Determine whether you want the rim of the sink to be set flush with the finish material (usually tile), set under it, or trimmed with quarter-round ceramic trim tiles.

If the sink is to be set flush, mount it on the surface of the plywood. The rim of the sink will usually be of the same thickness as the tile.

For a recessed rim, rout a groove around the edge of the sink opening, apply a bead of caulk or putty, and set the sink into the groove so the rim fits flush with the plywood. You can also suspend a recessed sink under the plywood top with mounting clips installed after the finish material is applied.

If the unit has an integral rim, apply a bead of caulk or plumber's putty around the edge of the countertop hole and set the sink into it.

If the unit has a separate metal rim, slip the rim onto the sink first and secure it carefully. Working from underneath, slip mounting clips into the rim and tighten them with a screwdriver to hold the sink in place.

Synthetic marble with rounded edges makes an attractive countertop that allows for an integral sink. It is sculpted to fit precisely and is easy to maintain.

Connect water supply lines to the shutoff valves. Hook up the drain. If the tailpiece does not fit into the P-trap, cut it shorter or add an extension piece. Before turning the water back on, remove the aerator attachment from the end of the faucet spout and leave if off for a few days. This will clear out any debris left in the pipes when the plumbing was roughed in.

WALL-MOUNTED SINKS:

A wall-mounted sink hangs on a bracket that is provided with it. Install the bracket according to manufacturer's instructions. Be sure to anchor it into the wall studs or into blocking installed between the studs. Use ¼-inch lag screws, 2½ inches long, or other heavy screws. Lower the sink down onto the bracket, making sure it catches securely. Straighten it with a level. Connect the drain and the water supply lines.

PEDESTAL SINKS:

The sink and pedestal are separate pieces. In some installations, the sink is hung on the wall first and the pedestal is installed under it. In others, the pedestal is installed first and the sink is set on top of it.

If your sink will be secured to the wall, make sure there is blocking between the studs. Instead of a bracket, many models are supported on heavy lag screws inserted through holes in the back of the sink. The pedestal is bolted to the floor. If you have to drill through tile to secure the bolts, use a special tile bit or carbide-tipped masonry bit.

Plumbing connections are the same as for other sinks, except you usually have more space to work in, and the fittings should be attractive. If the water supply lines show, use connectors of the smooth type rather than the flexible type to give a better appearance. Carefully shape them into a graceful arc or an S-curve using a tubing bender. Cut them to the correct length with a tubing cutter.

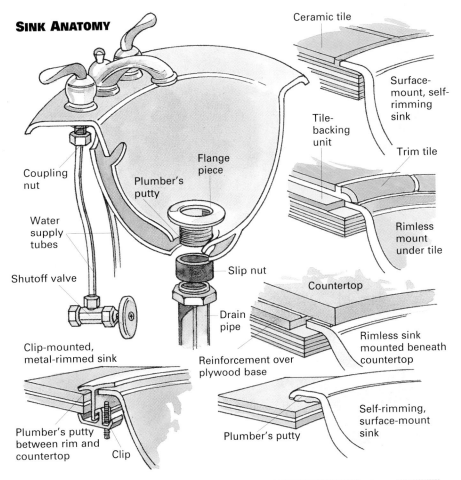

SINK ANATOMY

Ceramic tile

Surface-mount, self-rimming sink

Tile-backing unit

Trim tile

Rimless mount under tile

Flange piece

Coupling nut

Plumber's putty

Water supply tubes

Slip nut

Shutoff valve

Countertop

Drain pipe

Rimless sink mounted beneath countertop

Clip-mounted, metal-rimmed sink

Reinforcement over plywood base

Self-rimming, surface-mount sink

Plumber's putty between rim and countertop

Clip

Plumber's putty

A pedestal sink fits the clean lines of this white cottage-style bathroom. The sink complements the free-standing corner storage bureau.

INSTALLING FIXTURES
continued

TOILETS

The toilet is usually installed at the very end of the project, after walls are painted and the flooring (except carpet) is installed. Putting in a toilet is quite simple, no more complicated than taking one out. The technique varies with the model, so follow the manufacturer's instructions. Be sure the rough-in dimensions for the drain and the shutoff valve are correct for the new toilet. Before you start, remove the temporary cover from the floor flange. The flange should be screwed securely to the floor.

■ Turn the new toilet bowl (or the whole toilet if it is a one-piece model) upside down and rest it on a bed of old towels or padding to protect it. Place a new wax ring around the outlet, pressing it firmly into place. If the closet flange is recessed below the level of the finish floor, use a wax ring with a plastic extension sleeve. The sleeve should face up when the bowl is in the upside-down position. Apply a bead of plumber's putty or bathtub caulk around the bottom of the bowl.

■ Slip closet bolts into the slots beside the floor flange. Press plumber's putty around the heads of the bolts, if necessary to hold them.

This elongated water-saving toilet has a private niche that shares its sleekly rounded form.

■ Turn the toilet bowl right side up and set it in place on the flange, making sure the two closet bolts slide up through the holes in the base of the toilet. Twist the bowl back and forth and rock it slightly as you press it down.

■ Slip shims of water-resistant material (such as scraps of vinyl flooring) under the base to level the bowl. Place the washers and nuts on the closet bolts and tighten the nuts snugly. Don't overtighten them or you will crack the base. Cover the nuts with ceramic or plastic caps provided with the toilet.

■ Install the tank according to the manufacturer's directions. Most tanks come with rubber washers and gaskets that must be put on in the proper sequence to prevent leaks. The tank will be connected to the bowl with two or three bolts. Tighten them carefully so as not to crack either piece.

■ Hook a 12-inch water supply line between the shutoff valve and the inlet stub of the flush valve. Open the shutoff valve and let the tank fill up. Stop any leaks around the fittings by tightening the nuts where leaks occur. Flush the toilet and watch for leaks around the base. If possible, have someone watch from under the floor, where a leak may otherwise go undetected. A leak under the toilet means the wax ring has slipped out of place. The only solution is to pull up the toilet and start over with a new wax ring.

FINISHING WALLS AND FLOORS

Applying finish materials to the walls and floor may be the most satisfying part of the whole project. You can finally see what the bathroom is going to look like. Take care that the finishing work is done accurately. Use the correct materials and tools and take time to do a good job. You'll be looking at these surfaces for years to come.

WALLS

The most important consideration in finishing bathroom walls is to purchase materials that are suitable for use in a wet area. Check labels carefully. Don't be shy about asking dealers for recommendations.

For a bathroom, specify a waterproof variety of wallboard. Wallboard, the basic surface material for most walls and ceilings, can be finished or covered in a variety of ways. After joints are taped and covered with wallboard compound, the surface is sanded smooth or a layer of texture is applied. Smooth walls are desirable for easy maintenance or as a base for wallcoverings or tile. Textured surfaces create interest giving the walls a tactile dimension.

If you want smooth walls, apply at least three layers of wallboard compound over the taped joints and nail depressions, sanding lightly after each coat. To be absolutely sure of a flawless surface, shine a light along the wall at an angle to accentuate any shadows caused by depressions or bumps. Inspect skylight wells carefully; bright sunlight will reveal any variations of the smooth wall.

For a textured finish, experiment on scraps of wallboard to find an effect you like. Try placing texturing compound on a large trowel and skip over the wall with it so lumps of texture form a random pattern. Mixing silica sand into the compound first and thinning it slightly will help create a more uniform look. Vary this technique by splashing lumps of compound onto the wall, then lightly running a large wallboard blade over them to knock the lumps down to a uniform height. For rustic textures, use a glove or mitt to spread compound onto the wall by hand. Or use a long-napped paint roller with the compound thinned to a batterlike consistency.

PAINT: Walls and ceilings of most bathrooms are subject to constant moisture and humidity, so choose and apply paint carefully. Use a PVA (polyvinyl acetate) primer to seal new wallboard before applying the final coats of paint. Do not use an oil-based primer—it will raise the grain of the wallboard paper.

The finish coat can either be a semigloss latex or an oil-based paint with a satin or semigloss finish. Flat finishes hold stains and are more subject to wear.

The finish texture of the paint can be varied by using different brushes and rollers. Roller sleeves with a short nap, or foam rollers, produce the smoothest finish. Rollers with longer naps produce "orange peel" finishes. Special thickening agents can be added to the paint to create a stipple finish.

Seal new woodwork with an oil-based primer. If you paint with a roller, use a foam roller sleeve for a smooth finish with no fuzz. Use an oil-based finish coat or a high-quality latex semigloss enamel.

Previously painted surfaces must be clean, dry, and free of peeling paint. Wash them with TSP (trisodium phosphate), mixed according to package directions. If the surfaces are glossy, roughen them with sandpaper before washing them with TSP, so the new paint will adhere better.

Consult a knowledgeable paint dealer for other recommendations, and always follow directions on the paint can. Some paints cannot be thinned; some can be applied only in a limited range of temperatures; and some require a specific type of brush for application.

To estimate the amount of paint you will need, measure the wall and ceiling surfaces you need to cover. Multiply the width by the height of each wall, and subtract the area of windows, doors, etc. Your paint dealer or the instructions on the paint can will tell you how much area each gallon will cover.

WALLCOVERINGS: Choose bathroom wallcoverings with the same care used to choose paint. Avoid traditional paper wallcoverings, hand-painted papers, and natural fibers and fabrics (such as silk, grass cloth, or hemp). The most suitable wallcoverings for bathrooms are vinyls. Some are all vinyl, which are durable and easy to maintain, but may be limited in patterns. Vinyl-coated papers are common and have almost unlimited patterns, but the backing can tear easily. Vinyls with a fabric backing of polyester or cheesecloth are more durable. Expanded vinyls are useful for covering rough wall surfaces.

FINISHING WALLS AND FLOORS
continued

To estimate the amount of wallcovering you will need, calculate the area to be covered and add about 10 percent for waste and trimming. Most American products cover about 35 square feet per roll; European or metric wallcoverings cover about 28 square feet per roll. (A roll is a standard unit of measurement and may actually consist of two or three rolls packaged together.) Because dye lots or printing runs may vary, be sure to buy enough wallcovering for the entire job at one time. Check the rolls before installing to be sure colors and patterns match.

Ask the dealer for recommendations about preparing the walls. In most cases, the best method is to seal new wallboard with primer, then paint it with an oil-based topcoat, and apply sizing, available where wallcoverings are sold. You can apply wallcoverings directly to unpainted wallboard, but it will be impossible to remove the wallcovering at a later date without destroying the wallboard itself.

WOOD: Bathroom walls covered with natural wood create a warm, inviting feeling, but they must be finished carefully. Otherwise, the wood can expand and contract as moisture levels in the bathroom change. The wood can also rot over time or trap moisture behind it that can rot structural members. Improperly finished wood also attracts mold and mildew.

To prevent these problems, seal and paint the bathroom wall before covering it. Then,

No one wants a dreary bathroom. Even though it's located in an old house, this perky bath is fanciful and up to date.

using a water-resistant sealer, coat the back and any hidden grooves of each piece of wood before installing it. To minimize future problems, choose a durable type of wood, such as redwood, cedar, or cypress. Apply waterproof adhesive or corrosion-resistant fasteners, such as aluminum or stainless steel nails. Finish the exposed surface with a sealer and two or three coats of finish.

WALL TILE: Ceramic and stone tiles are installed in the same way. Tiles designated for use on walls are generally thinner than floor tiles. A successful installation depends on a smooth and stable backing that won't flex or deteriorate.

You can attach the tiles directly to the wallboard if the walls are firm and not exposed to direct moisture. Use a mastic recommended by the tile dealer. In a shower stall, tub surround, or other areas exposed to water, tile should be laid over a mortar bed installed by a professional or over special tile-backing units, which you can install yourself.

Some tile-backing units are made of cement with an outer mesh of fiberglass. Others are made of lightweight composite materials. They come in panels that are installed in much the same way as wallboard.

Cut them with a utility knife and nail them to the wall studs with galvanized roofing nails, or follow the manufacturer's instructions. Seal joints with fiberglass mesh tape and water-resistant joint compound or tile adhesive.

PLANNING A TILE PROJECT: Plan the layout carefully before setting any tiles. Don't just start setting tiles in one corner and work your way across the room. If you do this, the grout lines may not be level or plumb, and the last row of tiles may have to be cut to an awkward-looking size. You may also discover that the grout lines do not align with some other prominent horizontal feature.

To avoid these problems, you need to know whether the floor is level and straight, whether the corners are plumb, and whether there are any prominent horizontal lines with which the layout must harmonize. You also need to know how much space will be left at the end of each row.

If the space is narrow, add its width to the span of a full tile, divide the sum in half, and use this measurement to cut both the starting tile and the end tile so they will be equal.

There are several ways to plan the layout. One method is to first determine what prominent horizontal you want to align the grout lines with. It may be the floor, the top of the tub, a counter, or some other feature. Snap a level line across the wall at that point, using a chalk line. Measure the distance from this line, first to the bottom of the wall, then to the highest point the tile will reach. Divide each measurement by the height of one tile, including grout. This will tell you the number of full tiles you will need and the size of the remaining space that must be filled with cut tiles. Then decide where the cut tiles should go. Plan the vertical layout in the same way.

Another method is to plot a tile pattern on the wall. Some tile setters use a pair of compass dividers and a pair of layout rods to do this. The rods are strips of 1×2, one cut to the width and the other to the height of the wall. The procedure is as follows:

■ Measure the width of the wall. At the center, suspend a plumb bob on a chalk line from the ceiling to the floor. Snap a plumb line on the wall and snap two more plumb lines close to the edges of the wall. They will indicate whether the corners are plumb and where the narrowest measurement is.

Measure the height of the wall. Snap a level line across the wall at the center and snap two more level lines as close to the floor and the ceiling as possible. They will indicate where the floor and the ceiling are not level or even. With a square, verify the angles created by the layout lines are 90 degrees.
■ Set the points of the compass divider to the width of one tile, plus one grout joint (1/16–3/16 inch). Walk the divider along the layout rod that represents the width of the wall, marking as you go. The space left over at the end will indicate how wide the cut tile has to be.
■ If you want to balance the layout so there will be cut tiles of equal size at both ends, measure the last space, add the width of a full tile, and divide the result in half. Turn over the layout rod and mark that distance on each end. Reset the dividers to the full width of a tile and a grout joint and walk them along the rod again. The spacings should come out even with the last mark. Mark the spacings on the wall by holding the rod just below the lowest horizontal line and transferring the marks; then repeat at the middle and top lines. The marks should align with the center plumb line, but not necessarily with the two outside plumb lines.
■ Repeat the process for the vertical layout, unless you are not installing tiles all the way to the ceiling. In that case, you can skip the vertical layout because you can finish with a full row of tiles wherever you want.

■ If you are using special border tiles or trim pieces that are a different width from the field tiles, adjust the vertical layout rod accordingly. Mark the border tiles at each end of the rod and work out the spacings for the field tiles between these marks.

TILE SETTING: When the layout is complete, snap a chalk line for the first row of full tiles. Using the notched trowel recommended by the manufacturer, spread adhesive over a small area. Try not to obliterate any guidelines. Set the tiles into the adhesive one by one, pressing them down with a slight twisting motion. Keep the adhesive from piling up in the joints, and remove any excess immediately from the face of the tiles. Use plastic tile spacers to maintain a uniform distance between the tiles so the grout lines will be straight. Move up the wall, one row at a time, until you have installed all the field tiles.
■ Fit tiles around obstacles, such as faucets, by cutting notches with a pair of nippers.
■ When you have set all the field tiles, set the border, trim, and cut tiles. To measure for a cut, place a full tile upside down over the gap to be filled. Mark it, leaving space for grout lines at the top and bottom. Cut along the mark and install the tile with the cut side facing out.
■ Allow adhesive to set overnight. You can use tape to hold the tiles in place while it is setting. Do all the grouting—walls, floors, and countertops—at once (*see page 92*).

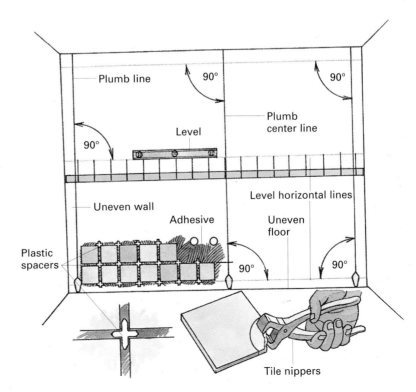

FINISHING WALLS AND FLOORS
continued

FLOORS

Make sure the subfloor is free of dust and debris. Also be careful about walking on the new floor while you're installing it. Most damage occurs during and just after installation, before the materials have settled.

TILE FLOOR: Ceramic and stone tiles are installed in the same way. Ceramic floor tiles are generally thicker than wall tiles. If you have to make many large or straight cuts, rent a tile saw (and wear safety goggles). Nippers will suffice for small trim jobs.

There are two ways to plan a layout for floor tile. The first is to start in the middle of the room, as described under Vinyl Floor Tile (*opposite*). The second method, described below, is to align the tiles with the doorway and with the most prominent wall at right angles to the doorway. You can try both methods and decide which one you prefer. Make sure the floor is clean, dry, and stable. Sand any rough surfaces and, if necessary, install an underlayment of particleboard or plywood at least ½ inch thick.

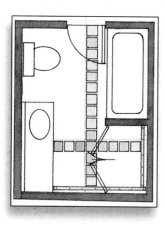

1 Snap a chalk line from the center of the doorway to the back of the room. Lay a row of tiles along the line. Remember to allow for the width of the grout. Mark the floor where the last full tile ends. Nail a strip of wood across the room so its inside edge is aligned with this mark, perpendicular to the original chalk line. The strip must be straight even if the back wall is not. Lay out a row of tiles perpendicular to the first row. Wherever the last full tile ends, nail down another strip of wood perpendicular to the first strip, forming an exact 90-degree angle.

2 Begin laying tiles at the intersection of the strips. Apply adhesive to the floor in two steps: First use the smooth edge of the trowel to help waterproof the underlayment; then comb the adhesive with the notched edge held at a 45-degree angle, covering one small section at a time.

3 Press each tile into place with a twisting motion. Use plastic tile spacers to keep the grout lines straight. Wipe excess mastic from the tiles immediately. Continue row by row until you have laid all the full tiles. Then remove the wood strips.

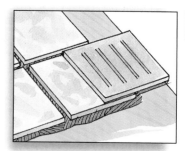

4 To fit around obstacles and along edges, first set each tile upside down over the gap it will fill. Mark the back, then turn the tile over and transfer the mark to the front. Cut with a tile saw, nipper, or rotary tool. To install cut tiles, apply mastic to the floor with a smooth trowel and to the back of the tile with a notched trowel. Press into place.

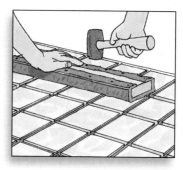

5 Press the surface with a floor roller or gently pound the tiles with a padded 2×4 and a mallet. Use scraps of plywood as knee boards to distribute your weight. This work should be done shortly after the installation.

6 Allow the adhesive to set for 24 hours. Apply the grout, using a rubber float. Spread it with diagonal strokes to keep the edge of the float from getting caught between the tiles. Tamp grout into all the crevices, using the handle of a toothbrush or a similar smooth tool. Wipe excess grout from the surface of the tile with a sponge, rinsing it frequently.

VINYL FLOOR TILE

Vinyl floor tiles are easy to install, but they must be laid carefully or water will get into the joints. The underlayment must be smooth, clean, and free of bulges. It is advisable to seal it with wood sealer or primer. Plan the layout carefully, as you would in planning a layout for ceramic tile. The following method will help you design a symmetrical layout. Compare it with the layout described on page 93 and choose the one you prefer.

1 Find the center of each of the four bathroom walls. Snap a chalk line on the floor between the center points of the north and south walls. Repeat the process with the east and west walls. The chalk lines should intersect at a 90-degree angle.

2 For even rows with identical borders: Lay one full row along either line without applying any mastic. If a space smaller than half a tile remains at the end, remove the last full tile. Measure the new space, divide the measurement in half, and insert a gap of that size at the beginning and end of the row. If the original space was wider than half a tile, leave it.

3 Set out a second row of tiles perpendicular to the first. Align this second row with the edges of the center tile in the first row, and set it as close to the second chalk line as possible. Use the procedure described in Step 2 to determine how to handle leftover space. Then move the entire first row until it is perfectly aligned with the second row. Snap new chalk lines to reflect the revised layout.

4 Using the mastic recommended by the tile manufacturer, set the four center tiles in place. Start with the quarter of the floor farthest from the door and fill it in with tiles. Apply the mastic to a small area at a time, to keep it from drying out and losing adhesion. Use only full tiles and work toward the walls in the sequence shown above. Cut tiles to fit around obstacles. If mastic rises between the tiles, wipe it off immediately with a damp rag.

Make a paper template of your floor's shape. In a larger room, lay the template over the sheet vinyl to guide your cutting. If you nail on baseboard molding, use scrap material to protect the new flooring and to elevate the molding slightly.

RESILIENT SHEET FLOORING: The underlayment for resilient flooring must be smooth, clean, and dry. This material is tricky to install because you must take care in cutting it to size and because a roll is heavy and unwieldy. Try to select a roll that is wide enough to avoid seams (widths up to 12 feet may be available).

■ Sheet flooring needs to relax before it is installed. Unroll it in a 70° F room and leave it spread out for at least 24 hours.

■ To cut a sheet to size, make a paper template. Tape together pieces of felt building paper until they entirely cover the floor. Leave an exposed perimeter of about ½ inch.

■ Hold a yardstick against the wall and scribe a line along the inside edge onto the paper. Continue until you have gone all the way around the room.

■ Carefully roll up the paper, take it into the other room, unroll it onto the new flooring, and tape it down. Align the design in the flooring with the edges of the pattern.

■ Hold a yardstick along the outside edge of the tracing line on the paper pattern. Scribe a line onto the new flooring along the outside edge of the yardstick. Repeat the process until you have gone around the entire pattern. Now you have a cutting line.

■ Cut out the flooring with a utility knife. Use a straightedge to guide it. Protect the floor underneath by working on a scrap of plywood or heavy cardboard.

■ Move the flooring into the bathroom and lay it out. Fold over half of the sheet to expose part of the floor. Spread mastic on the exposed floor and fold the sheet back onto it. Roll it with a floor roller, then fold back the other half of the sheet and repeat the process.

■ If you install baseboard molding, put a piece of cardboard under it as you nail it in place. This leaves room for the resilient flooring to expand. Cover the exposed edge at the doorway with a metal trim piece.

FINAL DETAILS

Accessories and finish details must be chosen carefully and installed straight and true so they enhance, rather than detract, from the overall effect.

TOWEL BARS

Installation techniques vary with the type of design. The best installations secure screws to wood framing behind the wall. Installing wood blocking between the studs, before the walls are closed in, is the most secure way to provide backing for the bars. Otherwise, use expansion bolts or plastic wall anchors to secure the screws where the brackets are installed between studs.

GRAB BARS

Unlike towel bars, grab bars are designed to support the full weight of a person. They attach to the wall with support flanges secured to the wall with screws. The screws must penetrate the wood framing behind the wallcovering, so it's important to install blocking between studs before covering up the walls.

Drill a pilot hole, smaller than the diameter of each screw. To drill through tile, use a tile bit or a bit with a carbide tip. It should be slightly larger than the diameter of the screw shank. Use a squirt bottle to train a steady stream of water on the bit as you drill to prevent overheating and to flush away tile particles. After drilling through the tile and backing, use the smaller diameter wood bit to complete the drilling into the wood framing.

If you are installing a grab bar in a shower or other wet area, apply a small bead of silicone caulking around each pilot hole before attaching the support flange. After screwing the flanges securely to the wall, slip the cover plate over each one and secure it with the set screw provided. Follow any other instructions provided by the manufacturer.

SHOWER DOORS

You can install shower doors for most standard tubs or simple shower stalls yourself, but doors that are integrated into full glass wall units should be installed by a professional. Most tub enclosures consist of two side rails attached to the walls, a top rail that rests on them and holds up the doors, and a bottom rail that provides a water barrier along the top of the bathtub rim. The bottom rail is usually installed first.

Begin by measuring the exact distance from wall to wall along the top of the bathtub rim. Cut the bottom rail to this length, using a hacksaw and miter box or a power miter saw with a carbide-tipped blade. Install the vinyl gasket or bead on the bottom of the rail and set it into place. Hold each side rail in place, making sure it interlocks over the bottom rail and is plumb. Mark the locations for the screws on the walls and remove the rails. Using the same techniques for drilling for grab bars, drill holes for the screws. Screw the side rails to the walls. Cut the top rail to length and set it down onto the side rails and hang the doors on it, as described in the manufacturer's instructions. Finally, run a bead of silicone caulk along the inside of each side rail where it meets the wall. Do not apply caulking along the inside edge of the bottom rail or water will not be able to flow under it back into the bathtub.

The door for a shower stall is installed with similar techniques. When installing the bottom rail, however, apply a bead of caulking inside the exterior edge to augment the vinyl gasket. Most models have a special sleeve on the side rail where the door is hinged so it can be adjusted to fit the exact width of the door opening.

ACCESSORIES

Soap dishes, toilet-paper holders, and similar accessories are secured to the wall with screws. They are not heavy enough to require solid-wood backing behind the walls, but where there is no wood backing, the screws should be secured with plastic wall anchors or expansion bolts.

Many toilet-paper holders are recessed into the wall and held in place by screws driven through the back of the housing. To accomplish this, cut a rough opening into the wallboard, then set the holder in place to test the size of the opening. Since there is nothing to which support screws can be attached, install a short 2×4 or similar blocking between the studs at the back of the rough opening. Secure it to the studs with screws or hold it in place with screws driven through the wallboard on the opposite side of the wall. Countersink and spackle the screw heads. Place the holder in position and secure it with screws driven into the new blocking.

INDEX

Boldface numbers indicate pages with photographs or illustrations related to the topic.

METRIC CONVERSIONS

U.S. Units to Metric Equivalents			Metric Units to U.S. Equivalents		
To Convert From	Multiply By	To Get	To Convert From	Multiply By	To Get
Inches	25.4	Millimetres	Millimetres	0.0394	Inches
Inches	2.54	Centimetres	Centimetres	0.3937	Inches
Feet	30.48	Centimetres	Centimetres	0.0328	Feet
Feet	0.3048	Metres	Metres	3.2808	Feet
Yards	0.9144	Metres	Metres	1.0936	Yards
Square inches	6.4516	Square centimetres	Square centimetres	0.1550	Square inches
Square feet	0.0929	Square metres	Square metres	10.764	Square feet
Square yards	0.8361	Square metres	Square metres	1.1960	Square yards
Acres	0.4047	Hectares	Hectares	2.4711	Acres
Cubic inches	16.387	Cubic centimetres	Cubic centimetres	0.0610	Cubic inches
Cubic feet	0.0283	Cubic metres	Cubic metres	35.315	Cubic feet
Cubic feet	28.316	Litres	Litres	0.0353	Cubic feet
Cubic yards	0.7646	Cubic metres	Cubic metres	1.308	Cubic yards
Cubic yards	764.55	Litres	Litres	0.0013	Cubic yards

To convert from degrees Fahrenheit (F) to degrees Celsius (C), first subtract 32, then multiply by $5/9$.

To convert from degrees Celsius to degrees Fahrenheit, multiply by $9/5$, then add 32.